Power Trip

By Don McCauley
A guide to weightlifting for coaches, athletes and parents

© 2010 Don McCauley

All Rights Reserved.

No part of this publication may be reproduced, stored in a retrieval system, or transmitted, in any form or by any means, electronic, mechanical, photocopying, recording, or otherwise, without the written permission of the author.

This edition published by
Dog Ear Publishing
4010 W. 86th Street, Ste H
Indianapolis, IN 46268

www.dogearpublishing.net

ISBN: 978-160844-446-5
This book is printed on acid-free paper.

Dedication -

To my Mother
To my Father
To my Wife
To my Family
To my Friends

Acknowledgements -

There are many people who have helped me write this book. Here are a few that have been of particular importance along the way.

Without them, my experience would not have been so complete or so much fun.

Uncle Bill McCauley, Tom Marchand, Walter Brown, Harold Bailey, Wayne Bailey, Keith Kenyon, Joe Dolce, Donna Ingham, Shin Ho Kang, Don Weideman, Dan Bell, Mark Cannella, Marty Schnorf, Kelly Pfitzer, and Mark Cameron.

And, two men twice missed: Jim O'Malley and Neil Wassermam

Sketches: Josh Beckler
Layout Design: Kelly Pfitzer
Pictured: Anthony Martin, Scott Dyer, Morgan and Alana Martin (cute kids) and Brian Kirkendall

Contents

INTRODUCTION 1
Chapter I: Q. and A. 5
   "What Are These Olympic-Style Lifts You're Talking About?" 5
   Why Should I Do These Lifts? 10
   Why should we listen to you? 10
   "We're Leaving at What Time?" 16
   Can We Prepare for the Trip Before We Leave the Driveway? 17
   Gas Station Fill-up 18
      Hey, what's that? 21
   Pot Hole 22
   What Do I Need for the Trip? 22
   Where Are We Going? 28
   Roadside Attraction 28
   Are there a lot of lifts I have to learn? 30
   What are the Best Techniques for Performing the Olympic-style Lifts? 35
      Answer #1: Use the "S" Pull 35
      Answer #2: Stay in the "POWER ZONE" 38
      Answer #3: Sweep the Bar 39
      Answer #4: Keep the "Launch Point" Close to the Hips 41
      Answer #5: Perfect the "Double-Knee Bend" 43
      Answer #6: Think of a "Power Circle" when You Lift 45
      Answer #7: Separate the unorthodox from the just plain wrong 46
   More about Getting to the Launch Point 47
CHAPTER II: PPaDftT-SM 50
   Preparatory Positions and Drills for the Ten-Step Method 50
   How Can I Learn Proper Technique? 50
   Gas Station Break 52
   Here's Where You Start to Learn Technique. 53
      The Warm up 53
   Just Standing Around Looking in a Mirror 54
   Gas Station 54
   Drill #1: Front, Back and Middle of the Foot Drill 55
   Drill #2: The Straight/Angled Back 56
   Drill #3: The Heel Jump 59
   Drill #4: Dirty Dancing 61
   Drill #5: Now, Up Against the Wall. 63
   How Should I hold the Bar? 65
      The Clean Grip Width 65
      Snatch Grip 67
   Where Do I Put My Feet at the Set Position? 68
   The Set Position 70
   Elbows and Shoulders and Hands 72
   Elbows 76

- Shoulders 78
- Quick Gas Station Break 80
- Deadend 80
- What are the 1st, 2nd, and 3rd Pulls? 81
  - The 1st Pull: Positioning the Bar 81
  - The 2nd Pull: The Catapult 82
  - The 3rd Pull: The Pull-Under 84
- CHAPTER III: The Ten-Step Method 86
  - Step 1: Full depth Air Squats 86
    - Quick Gas Station Break 89
  - Step 2: The Muscle Snatch 90
  - Step 3: The Overhead Squat 91
  - Step 4: The Drop Snatch 93
  - Step 5: Let's Rock and Roll*and Learn the Olympic Lifts 95
    - Part A 97
    - Part B 101
  - Step 6: Ready, Set and Sweep the Bar 102
  - Step 7: Partial Deadlift/Stop and Shift/Power Snatch 106
  - Step 8: Now, the Full Snatch (Squat-style) from the Launch Point, Hang and from the Floor 107
    - Full Squat Snatch from the Hang 108
    - Full Squat Snatch From the Floor 110
  - Step 9: Power Clean Rock & Roll 112
    - Part A 112
    - Part B 113
  - Step 10: The Full Squat Clean from the Launch Point 115
    - Full Squat Clean from the Hang 116
    - The Full Squat Clean from the Floor 117
  - A Quick Word about the Split Style 118
  - ROADSIDE ATTRACTION 119
- Chapter IV: Over Your Head 121
  - The Split Jerk, the Power Jerk and the Squat Jerk 121
  - Some Thoughts About the Split Jerk 123
  - The Split's Not Simple…But It's Easy 123
  - Staying Sane and Simplifying the Jerk Split 124
  - The Drive: The Jerk in the Box 126
  - Learning the Dip and Drive: What to Emphasize 130
  - A Little Trick to Stop Tipping when Dipping 133
  - Recovery from the Split Jerk Stance 135
  - Roadside Attraction 136
  - Rest Stop for Strength Coaches 138
- Chapter V: Man as a Machine 140
  - The Human Lifting Machine: Catapults, Cranes, Pendulums and Slingshots 140
  - The Cranes and the Pendulum 141
  - Positioning, Loading and Firing the Catapult 142
  - Fine Tuning the Catapult 143
  - Finally…the Slingshot 144

    Standing up 145
    The Twilight Zone Information Center 146
        The Olympic-Style Lifts/Triple Extension Myth 146
    Gas Station Break 148
    Is the "S" Tilting and Are Lifters Jumping Backward?? 148
    Are Those shoulders Set Behind the Bar? 149
    What About Pulling and Set Positions for Athletes in Other Sports?? 150
    Pop Quiz 152
CHAPTER VI: Nuts and Bolts 154
    Spotting and Physical Cues 154
    Spotting 156
    The Three Person Spot 156
    The Two Person Spot 157
    The One Person Spot 158
    Pulls (Drives): The Exercise 159
    Types of Pulls (Drives) 161
    A Bit More about Pulls from Blocks 164
    Lifts from the Blocks vs. Lifts from Hang 167
    "THE BIG 3" 168
    (1)The Power Clean & Jerk 168
    A Quick Note About the Next Lift 169
    (2) The Full Back Squat 169
    Back Squatting Basics 171
    The Olympic Back Squat Variation 173
    Low Bar Squats 173
    (3) Olympic-style Deadlifts 173
    Important Assistance Exercises 176
        Front Squats 176
        The Kang Squat 178
        The Romanian Deadlift 179
        The Overhead Squat 181
        Push Press 183
        Step-Ups 183
        The Lunge 185
        Good Morning 186
        Bent over Row 186
    And, for the Muscles in the Mirror 187
        Incline Press* 188
        Standing Shoulder Press 189
        The Bench Press 189
    Dumbbell and Kettlebells 191
    Abdominal Work 192
    So, Is That All There Is? 192
    And then, there is this. It's important. 193
Glossary 195
References 197

INTRODUCTION

Let's get something straight, right off the bat. For any of you coaching or competing in sports from football to golf, doing the Olympic-style lifts is essential. You'll notice I didn't qualify that statement with an "I think" or "Many believe" or some such dodge. No. This is not debatable; so let's just accept that as fact. By the Olympic-style lifts, I am referring to the following: Power Clean, Power Snatch, Power Clean & Jerk, Clean, Clean & Jerk, Snatch, all variations of those lifts from the hanging positions and from blocks and with dumbbells, Pulls of all types, Power Jerks, Split Jerks and Squat Jerks. Again, accept the need for some of these lifts in the weightlifting program you do for your sport as deeply as you accept the fact that you need air to breathe. They are critical for the serious athletes who want to increase their ability to produce powerful movements and to better endure the wearing affects of competition.

I want to insert this next bit of information here because it important for you to know and you don't have that much time, believe it or not. So-called strength coaches who do not emphasize the above lifts as a central part of their weightlifting program for athletes are simply derelict in their duties. If you are an athlete or a parent of one, you are being cheated of time and money if you waste a day doing a program that doesn't include some of the above-mentioned lifts. Now, you may be one of the lucky ones who has some money to waste, but I'll guarantee you that time is a commodity that all athletes have little of, even those who are so young that they don't consciously think of their physical abilities ever leaving them.

Don't be fooled. Many of these guys use a lot of gimmicks and their programs look pretty impressive. But, you can pull parachutes 'til you drop, stretch with cords, wave sticks around, do plyometrics, hop over baby hurdles and balance on wobbly boards or bouncy balls until sundown; if you don't do the lifts I've mentioned above as the core of your training program, you'll be an athlete who is all frosting and no cake.

If you have a problem with the above statements, you are probably going to get really angry as you read through the text of this book. So rather than get your panties in a twist, you may as well run like the wind and find another little manual that will make you feel all warm and fuzzy about the workout you're doing and one that won't be so free with the author's opinions about the state of sport and strength training. Good luck to you and your coach. Do me a favor though. Buy this book first. It'll make good, dry kindling for the next campfire you start, and I really need the money. Or, perhaps you can do some curls while you balance on it.

I am going to bring you on a road trip through the world of power/strength training. I'll tell you how to start and what to look for along the way. If you are preparing for competitive athletics, I will give you good advice about the specific weightlifting skills you will have to work on and the gear you will need. I'll discuss some of the equipment you won't find in a catalog that you might need to become a better weightlifter and some little tricks that might help you avoid or rid yourself of some common technique flaws. Using the companion DVD, you will get to learn by seeing and hearing how to perform these lifts and drills correctly.

I will help you avoid the inevitable Pot Holes, Dead Ends and Detours and try to keep you on the Power Highway, which is the most direct route to becoming a more powerful athlete. Along the way we'll also visit Rest Stops and Information Centers, where I'll give you a little heads up on the latest information about weightlifting techniques being used by the best weightlifters as well as my rationale for teaching the lifts the way I do. Occasionally, we'll stop at a Roadside Attraction for some diversion or a Gas Station to get directions or just have a few laughs. I'll provide a clearer idea of why you should do weightlifting this way, no matter what your sport, your age or whether you're an athlete learning or a coach teaching.

I am NOT going to give you a specific yearly program for weightlifting training for your sport. There are simply too many variations and there are good coaches who have a lot more experience than me in specific sports who have very good programs available in books and on video. I will, however, give you guidelines as to what you should be looking for in a program. This book's intent is to introduce you to the important weightlifting exercises and the latest information on technique, as well as some crucial assistance exercises.

I'm not going to spend a lot of time in this book writing about the developmental *holes* I believe most U.S. athletes have because of improper preparation for high level sports performance most have received. Let me just state this. If you are a pre-teen or teenage athlete who competes in four or five sports per year or unending competitive seasons, you are in an abusive situation, not athletics. If you haven't taken or been given time to run through the woods or streets and alleys with your friends, jump up on rocks, jump rope, wrestle anyone that came by, skate backwards, play hop scotch, bale hay or chop wood, climb trees, jump off a swing for height and distance, play dodge ball, climb over a fence, play sand lot football and do back flips and cartwheels for fun, you haven't been properly prepared for high competition levels in true power sports.

If you've already jumped on the yearly treadmill of one competitive season right after another, you, or your parents, are turning what should be the proper outlet for hard training, which is what competitions should be, into what amounts to an unhealthy psychological addiction and an abuse of your body. You should watch and try different sports to see what you like. That is being curious. I would advise you to pick one or two that you really, really like and work to get better at the techniques of one or both, and get physically prepared by training with weights and conditioning. The off-season is when athletes really prepare for competition. You'll never be prepared if you don't ever have one.

Weightlifting will not make you a more skilled athlete at your sport unless that sport happens to be Olympic Weightlifting. Natural ability and good, sport specific training both have an awful lot to do with the level athletes eventually reach. Without proper weightlifting from an early age, however, no athlete will reach close to his potential and many will fall prey to injuries that could have been avoided if they were strong enough to withstand the wearing affects of competition and training for competitive sports.

I hope you enjoy the trip.

Chapter I: Q. and A.
"What Are These Olympic-Style Lifts You're Talking About?"

For those of you unfamiliar with the term "Olympic-style lifts," I'm going to give a very quick explanation and show you some captioned pictures. The term "Olympic-style lifts," as I will define them in this book, describes (1) weightlifting movements during which the lifter utilizing strength, rhythm and agility quickly drives an Olympic bar, hopefully laden with weight, from the floor, blocks or a hanging position, to the shoulders or overhead, using the leg, hip, back and arm muscles in a coordinated effort, dominated by powerful hip extension. (2) Similar movements done with an Olympic bar, dumbbells or kettlebells lifted from blocks, the floor or a hanging position. (3) Pulls or drives, in which the athlete lifts an Olympic bar through a similar first phase of the lift from the floor, block or hang to the hip region and into the more accelerated second phase above the hips, but not to the shoulders or overhead.

Set Position
Power Clean/Clean-Start

Receiving Position
Power Clean-High Catch

*Receiving Position
Clean-Low Catch*

*Receiving Position
Snatch-Low Catch*

Clean Pull

The term Pulls has duel definitions in Olympic weightlifting circles. The above is the use of the term as an exercise that is done with substantial weight on the bar and is for extra strengthening.

Pull is also a term that is used to describe phases of the Olympic lift. You will come upon 1st, 2nd and 3rd Pull when you are reading about Olympic weightlifting in this and other books or listening to people talk about it. The 1st and 2nd pulls describe the ascent of the bar from its starting point and the 3rd pull actually describes the athletes accelerated descent to catch the bar before it falls back to the floor.

I have purposely used a wide-ranging definition of Olympic-style lifts, which are sometimes defined narrowly as the classic, competitive lifts - the Snatch and the Clean & Jerk. But in truth, many variations of the classic lifts are used in training and are all referred to as Olympic-style lifts. Power Cleans and Power Snatches, for instance, only differ from the classic lifts in the higher catch position used, not the basic form and rhythm of most of the lift.

I'm using my definition so a lot of you that aren't used to seeing or asking about Olympic-style lifts can come to see that there is a relationship between this whole group of movements and that Olympic lifts aren't just the ones you see the big guys doing on TV. I want you to understand that this whole group of lifts relates to all athletes' development for virtually all sports excluding, possibly, Thumb Wrestling and Rock-Paper-Scissors.

The complete Olympic-style lifts are comprised of what is generally referred to as a <u>First Pull</u> during which the athlete drives the bar from the floor or platform to the hip region at a medium pace, a <u>Second Pull</u> during which the bar is catapulted upwards mostly by a powerful hip extension, and a <u>Third Pull</u> called a Pull-under or Slingshot, during which the athlete propels himself downward to catch the bar before it falls to the floor.

Here are some photos that will give you some different views of what athletes look like during these lifts and also a bit of weightlifting jargon as well.

Mid 1st Pull

Start 2nd Pull

Start 3rd Pull

Power Snatch

Full Snatch-Squat Snatch, Snatch

Chapter I: Q. and A.

Full Clean, Squat Clean, Clean

Split Jerk

Start-Block Snatch

Power Jerk

Why Should I Do These Lifts?

If you believe that you need to be more agile and learn better balancing skills and be aerobically fitter but have a question about whether you should be weightlifting, listen for a minute. If I told you I had a vitamin/mineral/herbal elixir that, taken in proper dosage, could help you develop higher bone density, increase your tendon strength, safely help you burn more calories, help you stave off diabetes and osteoporosis, boost your self-esteem and make you stronger to boot, you'd buy a year's supply wouldn't you? Of course you would. You'd call that guy with a machine gun delivery on the infomercial as fast as you could.

Well, that's what weightlifting does. No, it doesn't stunt growth. No, it doesn't make kids muscle-bound. No, it won't make a women look like a man. No, it won't make you inflexible. No, it won't give you a hernia. No, it won't break your back. No, muscle doesn't turn to fat. No, it won't ruin your knees. In fact, if properly taught, weightlifting is an integral part of proper physical development and can not only make you physically and mentally stronger but it can help prevent many sports related injuries. If you continue a consistent and proper weightlifting program through and past your competitive career it can minimize those age related tormentors like bad back, bad knees and bad hips, as well.

Why should we listen to you?

Fair enough. You don't know me. I'm not a coach of any major college or professional team and I wasn't a star athlete. Why should you take my word for anything? Well, I have coached a few highly ranked weightlifters including an Olympic Team member, four World, Jr. World and Pan-Am Team members, two National champions and several medallists. I have also coached successful powerlifters. I coached some pretty good high school throwers in discus, shot, javelin and hammer, as well as football, baseball and basketball players. But I don't take many things on faith, and I'd be a bit hypocritical if I expected you to do that.

In lieu of having overwhelmingly recognizable coaching credentials in that I don't get a large salary or have a contract with a shoe company, let me present the results of a survey. I think it will give you a solid rationale for following the weightlifting path I suggest in this book and demonstrate on the DVD. This may not convince you to buy into everything I say but it may convince you to at least consider some of it.

I e-mailed and/or telephoned the strength and conditioning coaches of the top 30 NCAA Div. I college football programs in the country: 26 responded. I asked them 7 simple questions. This is certainly not a scientific survey. Anyone who knows anything about training athletes understands that there are many aspects to an overall program designed to enhance the many facets of strength and produce an athlete who is, in all measure, more powerful in movements such as squatting, deadlifting, upper body lifting, using medicine ball, throwing and lifting implements both balanced and unbalanced, plyometric exercises, running drills and lots more. However, as far as what is done in the weightlifting area, I think this demonstrates that things have certainly taken a turn towards the use of the Olympic-style lifts in these programs over the last quarter century.

Here are the survey questions.

1. Do you use the Olympic-style lifts (or variations) in your program?
2. Do you use the Power Clean?
3. Do you do hang or block Cleans (or power versions)?
4. Would you consider the Olympic-style lifts a major part of your weightlifting program?
5. Do you consider the Olympic-style lifts more important than the bench press?
6. Do you do full squat cleans in your program?
7. Do you have athletes do full (hip joint below knee joints) back squats?

Here are the results.

In the quick and dirty summary, 94% of the top 26 responding strength and conditioning coaches answered a resounding **YES** to questions # 1-4. In answering question # 5, which I (very unscientifically) put in there to see if it would finally put the last nail in that coffin, **97%** of the coaches said the Olympic-style lifts are more important for athletic development than the bench press (some coaches chuckled), while the latter is certainly a good exercise for upper body strength.

Sixty percent (60%) of the coaches preferred the above parallel catch position (Power) when athletes performed the Olympic-style lifts, while twenty five (25%) used a below- parallel catch position (Squat) in their programs with some coaches in the first group saying that the above-parallel catch (Power) position is more useful for their sport's athletes. The remaining coaches didn't have as strict a requirement for the catch position, some using the squat position only in the teaching phase of their program, and some allowing it in the testing phase and some preferring it outright.

Full Squat Clean   *Power Clean*

Power Snatch   *Squat Snatch*

I will add here that when I was talking to these coaches I seldom got the impression that most were so rigid about this catching technique (receiving position) that they would stop an athlete who was proficient at doing full squat cleans or snatches from using this technique if he wished. The critical goals these coaches had in common were to get their athletes doing these olympic-style lifts and doing them correctly.

A full 89% of the coaches said outright that when doing Back Squats they encouraged <u>full Back Squat</u> positions (hips below knees at lowest position) for their players, with several saying they let athletes go as low as they could. All but one of the remaining coaches described their squats as parallel but said that that the line they used was along the top of the quads (which normally puts the hip joint below the knee joint, anyway). One coach said that he does not require athletes to squat as low as parallel.

Below parallel-correct   *parallel-incorrect*   *above parallel-useless*

The only significant difference of opinion concerning the survey questions among these coaches had nothing to do with whether or not to do these lifts but whether or not to use the low catch position in the normal day-to-day training of these football athletes. Back Squats, for the vast majority of coaches programs were done below parallel and the bench press was basically put in its realistic place in these strength and conditioning programs.

This was a short survey and doesn't cover the totality of any of these programs. All the coaches involved will have their own ideas about intensity and volume, and all have many of their own unique ideas about which exercises appropriate for their athletes strength, agility, quickness and conditioning. These are football strength and conditioning coaches (although some supervised all or several sports), so you may ask, if you are a soccer or a baseball or a basketball player, why this information should apply to you?

I would say this to you. Fully developing your potential for power, in its various forms, is something that all athletes have in common and these Olympic-style lifts are simply far superior weightlifting movements for doing that. So, whether you are a soccer player, a football player or a tennis player, the core of your weightlifting training should only differ in measure, not in kind.

On another matter, I will take the position in this book that the above-parallel catch position (Power) fulfills the needs of the athletes competing in most sports. The below-parallel (Squat or Split) position is required in only a few sports. Olympic weightlifting, MMA, CrossFit , free-style wrestling, gymnastics and the martial arts are examples of these sports. Some specific player positions in some sports like hockey and soccer goalies also have a critical need of this skill.

My reasoning is as follows: I believe most of the benefit of using the Olympic-style lifts and variations comes from a tremendous increase in hip extension power output, unmatched development of the muscles of the posterior chain, especially back, glutes, hamstrings, unparalleled enhancement of the athlete's ability to perform triple extension movements, and the quick ankle, knee, hip and shoulder joint coordination used to catch the bar in the higher-above parallel- position.

Learning to accelerate explosively downward is also a great benefit of Olympic lifting. Accelerating down to a full squat, however, isn't a skill that correlates to movements in many sports. Most athletes play their sports in a partially flexed, upright position and engage opponents, deliver blows or throw some implement from that position. Power Cleans and Power Snatches, from the explosive acceleration to the above-parallel receiving positions are more similar to the playing positions of most athletes and are simply more appropriate for most. Even football linemen, who may start in a low, hip-flexed position, extend their hips to a partially upright position and attempt to operate from it or drive almost horizontally (drive blocking) using forceful hip extension. There is no accelerated return to the lower flexed position (full squat or split), so I don't propose that they spend a lot of time learning how to get there.

A good number of weightlifting coaches disagree. They take the position that learning and using the full squat (low catch) is best because it is a more complicated neuro-muscular skill and will reap eventual benefits for all athletes. They believe that it is essential for athletes to learn this movement if they use the Olympic-style lifts in their strength and conditioning program. They believe that the athlete will gain so much from the use of this skill in body awareness and flexibility that it will translate to their field performance better than just learning the high position catch. I don't believe that but it is worth your consideration.

Whichever catch position your strength coach wants you to learn; you are an athlete with a happy problem. Either way, your coach is having you do the Olympic-style lifts and that will be of such great benefit to you as an athlete, the method you use in catching the bar is much less important.

Let's get back to your reasons for reading this book and watching the DVD. While you still don't know much about me, you should conclude that these NCAA coaches, who have a great deal to gain or lose and have the opportunity to learn and weigh the best information available, might be in such uniform agreement for a good reason. By an overwhelming majority, they prescribe many of the lifts that I will describe to you in this book. Why in the world would you waste your time doing things a lot differently than these coaches suggest? They are arguably working with athletes in the most popular team sport in the U.S. They work with a huge volume of the most critiqued, tested and, simply, some of the best athletes in college level sports. It would be illogical to think that, with all the information now available to them and so much at stake, so many of them would follow a path that lessened their athletes' chances to reach their potential. I propose that you should give some serious consideration to the path that these coaches take in training athletes and whether or not it is based on any real science.

One of the common complaints I hear from college strength and conditioning coaches is that they have to spend an inordinate amount of time teaching newly arriving athletes these Olympic-style lifts. This causes a significant loss of time before any benefit can be derived from doing the actual weightlifting program. Many athletes, even the very good ones, haven't done these lifts in the past or have been taught to do them incorrectly and must play catch-up. This is a tragic waste of time. These athletes have been put years behind where they should be in strength, power and technique development by not having done these lifts for at least ten years prior to college age. I suggest that you learn these lifts as soon as possible and not have to play catch-up with those who have.

"We're Leaving at What Time?"

As much as I hate admitting that doing anything (even waking up) early is good; chronologically early is when to start your Power Trip. So, here we go. Get in the car. Mom, you're driving.

*****

Parents or coaches of four, five and six years old should be teaching their kids to do agility drills, balancing skills, sprinting and weightlifting right along with aerobic conditioning through play or play-like programs. If they are already playing soccer, football, baseball, or some other competitive sport, they should be learning these other skills as well. If they don't, they will have some of those holes in their skills that I mentioned earlier. Although some will do better than others at competitive sports because of natural gifts, all of them should fill these holes early because it gets very difficult to fill them later. It might not be possible at all. And that will affect whether they will ever reach their full potential for power or the specific skill level required in sports.

We used to fill in a lot of these holes in ancient times by doing a very odd thing we called playing. Your kids don't do much of that anymore and that's why they are weak, fat, and very unhealthy physically and mentally. Don't take offense here. Fix it. The fact that most of them have played video games and have not climbed a tree is certainly one of the early signs of the fall of western civilization, as we know it.

I'm not going to put yet another major guilt trip on you parents out there. It is not the same world today as the one in which I grew up. It is, in fact, damn scary out there. Most of you cannot let your kids go out and play for hours on end and count on them coming back when you call them for dinner or when the streetlights come on. There are video distractions galore to keep kids immobile in their rooms and on their butts. Somehow, you must get them up and out. What I will say to you is something you should really know already.

You are the first and most important teacher your child will ever have. If you read to your child early, she will learn to read and enjoy reading. If you play with your child early, he will learn to play and enjoy playing. Do both and your child will know how to find answers to questions and will want to be physically active for life. These are great gifts to give any child and well worth your effort. Get to it.

*****

Can We Prepare for the Trip Before We Leave the Driveway?

Here are a few simple ideas that don't take up a lot of space or cost a lot of money and can be directed by any Mom or Dad coach:

Do you remember how your child used to sit in a deep, flat-footed squat when he/she was two or three years old? Well, if your child can still do that, have him hug a big ball (basketball will do) and do that kind of squat. When he gets up, have him throw or bounce the ball to you. Bounce or throw it back and have him do another full depth, flat-footed squat. Do this for about ten minutes and then both of you can go have an apple or another treat for a reward. Kneel down and get to your kid's level and, by all means, play with your child. Young children will train for sports when they are ready to, not before.

Let's talk a bit more here about squatting. Do all sort of squats with your children: air squats, overhead squats with a PVC dowel, squats with a ball, etc. This is as much a preparatory skill as jumping or hopping and is overlooked by most programs.

Lateral Jumps   *Front/Back Jumps*   *Fast Jump Rope*

Overhead squats w/PVC bar   *Cute Kid*

A line on the floor (or a broomstick) creates the simplest agility drill "equipment." Simply have your child jump forward and back or side to side over it. They can start doing it with two-footed hops and then a single-footed hops. Then, do zigzag hops over and back. Then hop over the line, reversing in mid air.

Here's another game that is great initial agility teacher.

Playing Hop Scotch with my cousin was my first agility and balance "drill." You can teach this simple game to your child at almost any age after they are walking.

Gas Station Fill-up

Very short and very simple advice:

- Teach your child to jump rope.
- Teach your child how to do a two-footed jump up onto a 3", 6", 12" box.
- Teach your child to back-pedal correctly.
- Teach your child to somersault forwards and backwards.

*****

The following is an idea stolen (with thanks and respect) from a very bright guy named Avery Faigenbaum who has a great weightlifting program with pre-adolescent kids. His weightlifting program is one of those **EUREKA!** ideas that is so simple it's brilliant. I suggest that every parent buy his books and incorporate some of his ideas in any program you want your child to do. He's a lot smarter than I am and has about ten times my energy. He has many great ideas about how to incorporate resistance training with different implements into your child's physical health program. Anyway, on to the "first barbell."

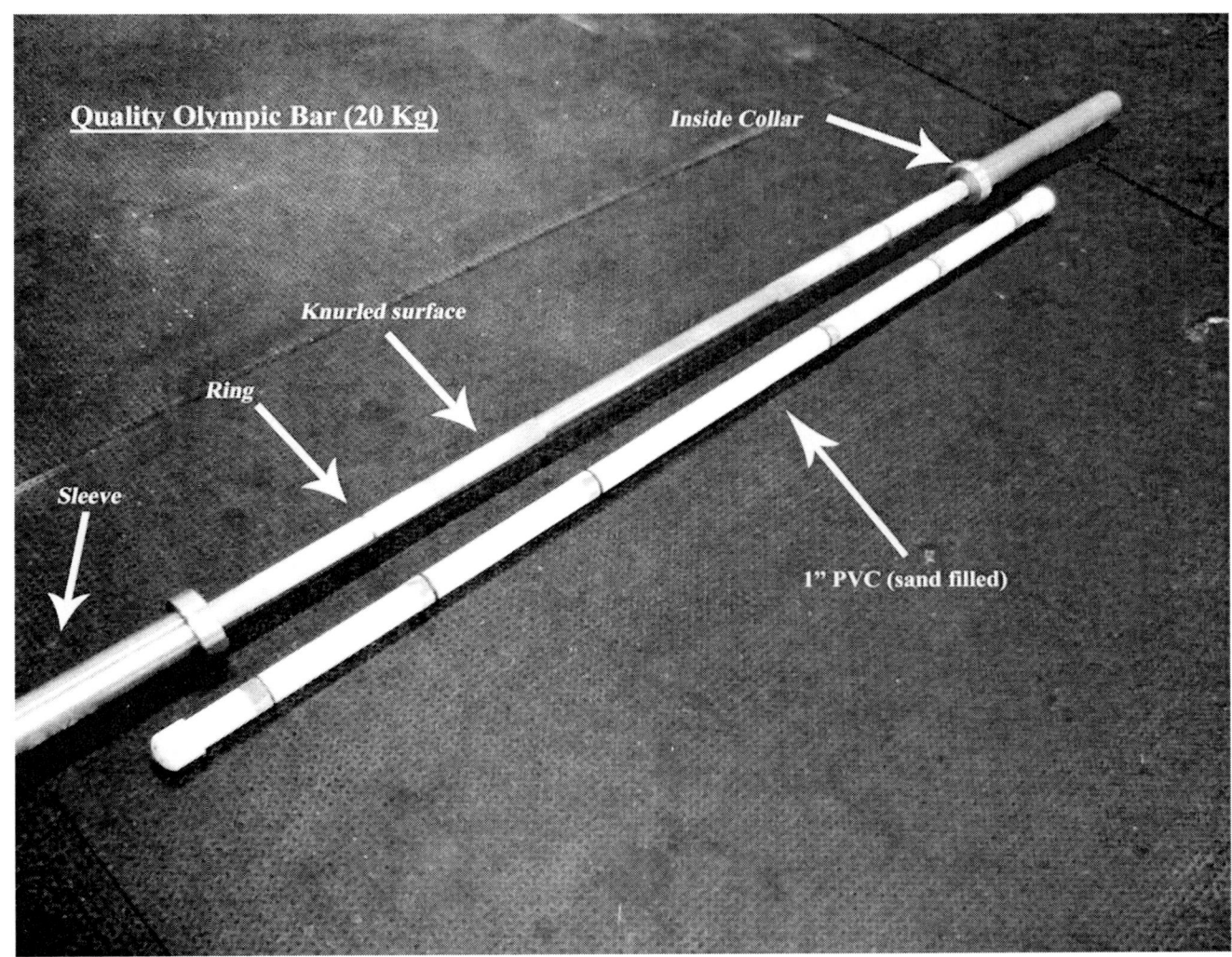
Olympic Bar and PVC Bar

Buy a five foot length of one inch diameter PVC pipe, some fine gravel, and a couple of PVC end caps to cover the ends of the PVC pipe. Put enough gravel into the pipe to fill about 1/4 of its length, glue the end caps onto the ends of the pipe. The great thing here is that when your child does the fast lifts correctly, the "barbell" makes a sound like a giant rattle.

For those of you who like science, by making that noise, it takes advantage on one of the best learning pathways we have: hearing. In addition, your child will feel the gravel move in the pipe using yet another pathway of learning. That's very important because during correct technical performance of many lifts, the athlete cannot be looking at the bar. Thus, simple is brilliant.

You can start teaching your young child some of the easier lifts or drills you see in the rest of this book and on the DVD. You can teach him about the Shoulder Press, the Full Squat, the Jerk and many of the others. And you can get him used to the names of all of these lifts so that when he's in high school he'll probably know more about them than his coaches. There is no excuse for not teaching a young child to move his body quickly and gracefully (except that you may have to run faster to catch him).

*****

If you start looking for more formal programs for your children to get into better shape or to get better prepared for competitive sports, I suggest to you that you enroll them in some sort of a basic gymnastics-training program. The basics of tumbling and other gymnastics movements should be learned in early childhood.

Another option is a new and exciting program that I think is just about the best formal program out there for kids is CrossFit for Kids. The CrossFit system of training incorporates Olympic lifting, weightlifting for strength, med ball, kettlebell, dumbbell movements, basic gymnastic movements and calisthenics, as well as aerobic training. One of the unique things about this CrossFit system is that the workouts are competitive to an extent. They are short and they are fun. I suggest this above all other organized programs because it is play-like (kids, on their own, are almost always competitive when they play) while teaching kids skills they really need, and it involves all energy systems of the body. You can use this system of training to ready your kids for a specific competitive sport or just to improve their fitness throughout pre-adolescence. And, because the program is based on self-improvement, it is a tremendous tool in building that elusive trait: self-esteem. This makes it a very attractive program to use as one part of anybody's *Power Trip*.

*****

I will point out here that CrossFit training may not be perfect for all sports as the athlete reaches high school level sports and above. The body's energy systems must be trained in specific ways for specific sports. Usually that means a huge over-emphasis of one or another of those systems to meet some requirement of the specific sport. This may mean doing lower repetitions of exercises during sets and taking rest breaks between these sets during most training sessions

Doing only CrossFit training all year for some sports would keep you very well-conditioned overall but may not allow you to keep (or gain) the body mass or the single maximum power output ability you might need for the highest levels of performance in those specific sports. In sports like football or throwing the shot, discus, hammer or Olympic weightlifting, for instance, extra muscle mass is a requirement, as is the ability to produce a single, huge burst of power. Training solely with CrossFit would not be the best prescription to add and keep this amount of mass or producing a single, maximum power bursts critical for those sports.

I highly recommend, however, that all of you do some CrossFit training within your training year because of the variation of exercises and high level of fitness, agility, power and strength gained by doing it. I have started using it with my Olympic weightlifters and am very pleased with the results. I recommend CrossFit highly as an overall conditioning program for children, teenagers and adults, whether or not they're participating in sports. It is an especially well designed program for police, firefighters and military people who must have a high level of all around conditioning and be able to respond at any given moment to a variety of physical challenges that may really mean life or death.

I will also say this about CrossFit in regards to its usefulness for many sports at all levels. With a few sport-specific modifications, CrossFit is superior to the programs being used for conditioning and weight training athletes in sports such as wrestling, boxing, MMA, judo, jujitsu, karate, gymnastics, rugby, lacrosse, long distance running and perhaps sports like basketball, baseball, tennis, soccer, swimming, diving and skating.

*****

So, now you've gotten your child off to an early start with some basics. That's all well and good, but what if he slept in? If he or she has started late, don't do a lot differently. Work on agility and conditioning first. Have them get the basics of weightlifting down, which you'll do if you stick with it and read this book. And, don't waste any more time. If your child is ten to twelve, it might be better to get him into an organized program run by professionals. Kids at about this age might consider playing with Mom or Dad boring, embarrassing or even cruel and unusual punishment. However, if your kids don't mind, go to it. But, keep in mind that kids of about this age will start to want more contact with other kids and less with you. Oh, I'm sure it won't happen to you, specifically, but to those other poor parents… Yeah, right.

Hey, what's that?

*****

Pot Hole

Dear teenage athletes,

The biggest problem you're going to encounter if you've gotten into these drills late is your own egos. You teenagers may have a big problem. It goes something like this in your heads: "I don't want to look like a fool or be caught playing Hop Scotch or some such nonsense and so I'll skip that sort of thing and go right on to the grown-up stuff." BIG MISTAKE. Start at the beginning. Fall on your butt. And, laugh at yourself. But, get up and do it again until you know how to move and control your body in all directions. And, by all means, go climb a tree if you haven't ever done that. You will not be able to efficiently produce the explosive acceleration and have the rhythm and agility you need in any competitive sports until you go out and play once in a while. Don't let your ego make you a proud fool.

Regards,
  Old coach

*****

What Do I Need for the Trip?
(To the athletes)

Besides a good sense of humor, there is only a small amount of equipment you need for this trip. We have just talked about some drills you can do to start off, but now we have to equip you and your "vehicle" for the longer trip. The good news is that most of the gear is cheap and lasts a long time. The rest of the equipment needed for the trip should be in the gym or training room you use. (Your <u>gym is your vehicle</u> for the purpose of sticking to the book's theme and your <u>personal gear</u> <u>is your luggage</u>. Both have to be complete to make it a good trip)

Your stuff:

1. Sweatpants, loose shorts, hat, underwear, socks, sweatshirts and t-shirts. Don't wear expensive poly-something pants to lift weights. The knurling on the Olympic bars will tear them to expensive shreds.
2. Straps - cotton, nylon or leather loops of material to be placed around the lifter's wrists and secured between the hands and the Olympic bar in

order to increase grip strength while doing heavy pulls, lifts or repetitions of certain versions of the Olympic-style lifts.

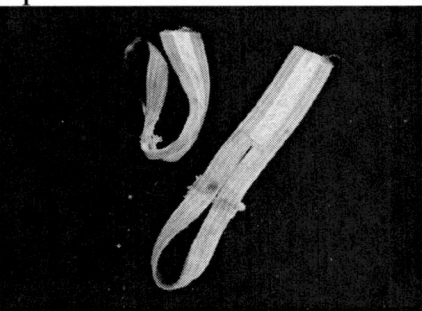

3. Good weightlifting shoes and a weightlifting belt.
4. Knee wraps (poly. sleeves are best)
5. A towel and soap for showering.
6. Athletic tape (for wrists and fingers)

Your gym should have:

Good Olympic bars and Light training bars.

Bumper (rubber) plates and metal as well

Platform (for Olympic lifts)

Blocks (for partial pulls or lifts)

Jerk Box

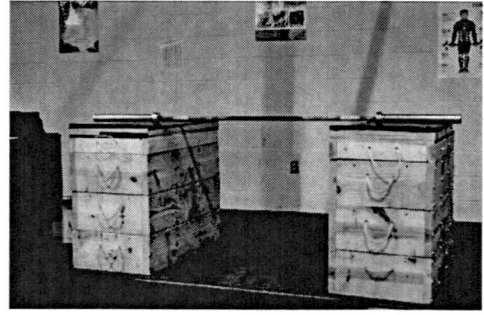

Med Balls

Bench Press Bench

Dumbbells

Adjustable Angle Bench

Squat Racks

Chapter I: Q. and A.

Jump Boxes

Glute/Ham Bench

Open sprinting and
 jumping area (outside is fine)

Jump Rope

Kettlebells

Resistance Bands

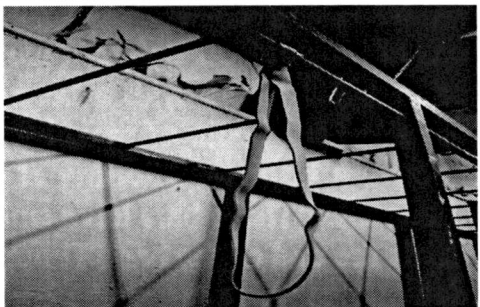

Qualified Coach (CrossFit, USAW, NSCA may be best)

Collars for securing weights on bars

Before we move on, here is some information about the "Olympic Bar" pictured above. This type of bar is familiar to most of us who have lived with weightlifting, but parents and young athletes might not be aware of what it is.

The classic "Olympic bar" refers to a steel weightlifting bar that weighs 20Kgs. (~45lbs.) and is 2.2 meters (~7 feet) long. It has thick "sleeves" at either end (see pic.- Pg. 19) on which the weight discs (plates) are loaded. The steel bar travels through these sleeves, and with the help of ball bearings or some other magical devices, it spins within them freely. This allows the bar to rotate in an athlete's hands when lifting it to his shoulders or overhead. This bit of engineering makes the lightening fast transitions seen in Olympic weightlifting possible. These bars are also a bit "springy" or elastic and will bend momentarily when enough weight is loaded on the ends or when an athlete delivers significant force to a heavily loaded bar changing its position or direction. This effect can be seen most readily in a lift called the Jerk, which you will see demonstrated on the DVD.

Much of the steel bar between the sleeves is scored in a criss-cross fashion, called knurling. This provides lifters with a better gripping surface when lifting. There is also a smooth portion in the middle of most bars where the bar will rest on the lifter's shoulders. Some bars have a bit more knurling at the center to attempt to provide a better hold across the collarbones. These bars have smooth "rings" that are small breaks in the knurling and are towards the end of the bar. These are used as general landmarks for athletes when they put their hands in place to grip the bar.

There are now lighter versions of the Olympic bar (pictured above) that are used by women and young athletes in competition weighing 15 Kgs. (~33lbs) and even lighter bars used for training novices and for warm-up purposes. Ten and even five kilogram bars are available. These are a must for younger lifters.

Chapter I: Q. and A.

To tell you the truth, you don't need much more to take this little road trip to **Power City**. In fact, there have been many athletes who have made the trip with a lot less. The only thing that you need that's not on this list is perseverance. Oh, and you should clean your gym clothes often. That's good for health and popularity.

Wait a minute. It's time for another quick turn.

*****

- If most of those things aren't available to you, you are NOT in a gym equipped to train athletes.
- If your gym has a lot of pretty machines but little in the way of "free-weights," then you are NOT in a gym equipped to train athletes.
- If there are no platforms, Olympic bars, chalk or bumpers in your gym, then you are NOT in a gym equipped to train athletes.
- If they don't allow you to drop weights (bumpers), lift overhead or use chalk in your gym, you are NOT in a gym equipped to train athletes. (Buy weights and use your garage, if you have to.)
- And, most important, if the driver (trainer, coach) isn't very good at your gym, you are NOT in a gym equipped to train athletes.

*****

Where Are We Going?

If you haven't noticed so far, I have a strong opinion about the value of the Olympic-style lifts as the core of any weightlifting program for any athlete in power sports, which includes all sports from Olympic weightlifting to football to golf.

On this **"Power Trip"** you're going to learn how to do these lifts correctly by using what I consider the most efficient method used today. You're also going to learn a little bit about why certain techniques of moving the bar through space are better than other techniques that are still used. You're going to learn that some things out there are simply trash littering the highway and interfering with your best chance to be as powerful an athlete as you can be. I'm going to help you find a proper place to work out, teach you to do the correct things when you get there and help you maximize your ability by simply making you a strong, smart athlete.

*****

Roadside Attraction
(for Football Coaches)

For a moment I'm going to talk to many of the high school football coaches in the U.S. about proper weightlifting for your sport. **YOU DON'T KNOW HOW TO DO IT.**
It's not really your fault. Most of the people you learned it from didn't know how to do it either, and they passed their "expertise" on to you. Find out how to do it correctly (this book will help), or hire someone who knows how to do it, and allow him to implement a workout plan for your athletes that makes sense. If Olympic-style lifts aren't central to your program, turn around and get on the right road. You're lost and you don't know it yet. You're going to get beaten by teams that aren't lost.

If you think the techniques of weightlifting are any less exact than those of your sport, you are mistaken. You don't just say "throw up a few power cleans" any more than you just tell an offensive guard to "just get up and run around the left side" when you're teaching him to pull and lead a running play, or you tell a defensive line just to "plug up the middle." Learn what the best lifts for your athletes are and how to teach all the lifts for your sport correctly or go hire someone who already knows what they are and how to do that.

Back to the road.

*****

I could fill this book with a lot of charts and graphs *proving* to you that doing the Olympic style movements will do more for you than anything else you could do in a weightlifting program to improve your power potential. But I've learned over the years that tests can be devised to prove just about anything. And, I find charts and graphs boring as hell and I'm not going to inflict a lot of them on you.

The information you need to know pertaining to the Olympic-style lifts is that when athletes perform them, they produce more than twice the measurable power output than in any other weightlifting exercise. Even the heavy-load exercises like back squats and dead lifts can't come close. Sport scientist, John Garhammer's work put an end to any realistic debate about the relative usefulness of the Olympic-style movements to other lifts for training athletes.

Simply, the Olympic-style lifts have to be the central feature of any athlete's weightlifting program. Many other lifts and drills make up all well balanced programs. Programs that emphasize the use of other major lifts like bench press, dead lifts and squats are, quite simply, lacking. While all these exercises are needed in almost all programs, without the Olympic-style lifts leading the way, you are becoming a tractor instead of a racecar. And, human racecars win in sports competitions.

So, if you want your weightlifting program to make you more powerful, do weightlifting exercises that produce more power. Do other exercises that will stabilize your body's core, such as full back squats, deadlifts or bent over rows, but base the core of your program on the exercises that teach your body to maximize its' power potential. Always remember: Power = force x distance/time. For our purposes, "distance/time" means SPEED. And, we all know what speed does in the competition arena, don't we. Remember, the Olympic-style lifts are FAST. **VERY FAST!**

Athletes who do these Olympic style lifts hit holes faster, jump higher, tackle and block harder on the football field than those who don't, and they do it for a longer time during games. They throw farther in field events. They run faster in all directions with higher efficiency and more game-specific endurance in all sports. They do better than athletes who do programs that don't include the olympic-style lifts. In any fairly equal competitive situation, I'll take the athletes who did these Olympic-style lifts over ones who didn't every time.

Note: This doesn't mean that you shouldn't do the other strengthening lifts and speed drills, by the way. They are important movements and some amount of them should be done in every athlete's program as well. But if hip extension ability is less than it can be, the rest of the body will deliver a second rate effort. And, Olympic-style lifting is the major way you can affect the muscles used in explosive hip extension. Nothing else comes close. There is no substitute.

Now, you know what to do. However, you have 3 more important questions to ask and have answered.

- Are there a lot of lifts I have to learn?
- What are the best techniques for performing the Olympic-style lifts?
- How can I learn proper technique?

Read on and you'll find your answers. Plus, you will see some really good pictures of men and women demonstrating proper positions in these lifts.

Are there a lot of lifts I have to learn?

Here are basic pictures of these lifts. For a better idea of what these lifts look like, play the DVD along with your readings. I have included more of the lifts and pulls here (driving the bar from the floor) than most of you will ever need to use in your sports careers. For some sports, only a small portion of these lifts will ever be needed. But, for all sports, some of these will be needed.

1. Power Clean

2. Power Snatch

3. Clean

4. Clean and Jerk (classic Olympic lift)

5. Snatch (classic Olympic lift)

6. Power Clean from Hang

7. Power Snatch from Hang

8. Clean from Hang

9. Snatch from Hang

Chapter I: Q. and A.   33

10. Power Clean from Blocks

11. Power Snatch from Blocks

12. Clean from Blocks

13. Snatch from Blocks

14. Split Jerk from Box/Racks (front or back)

15. Power Jerk from Box/Racks (front or back)

16. Clean Pull (full)

17. Snatch Pull (full)

18. Football Power Drive (full extension and arm involvement)

There are other variations, but these are the major ones used by most sports. Also, there is another method of catching the bar called a Split, which can be used instead of the semi or full squatting positions shown above.

What are the Best Techniques for Performing the Olympic-style Lifts?

There are a few basic things that you have to use to perform these Olympic lifts the way they are done today. And, there are a couple of things that you should think about when you are performing these lifts. Here they are.

Answer #1: Use the "S" Pull

Let's get this out of the way early. When pulling (driving) the bar from the floor to the shoulders or overhead, the best way to get from point A to point B is NOT, NOT, NOT a straight line. This is important for you to know. It is as true as is the value of these Olympic-style lifts in the first place. It is NOT debatable.

You will hear coaches who talk about a so-called "straight pull," which is ok if you happen to be living in the 1940's. Weightlifting technique has evolved and the straight pull is a dinosaur (except in the U.S.). A straight line is no better at moving a bar from the floor to the shoulders than launching a rocket from the Earth to the Moon.

Some coaches still insist that a straight pull is preferable, in the face of the fact that the **"S"** pull is used by 99.9% of the international class athletes competing in Olympic Weightlifting, in which the major goal of the athletes is to lift the most weight using the classic Olympic lifts! I believe that all athletes from all sports who learn the Olympic-style lifts should be taught the "S" pull, whether or not they are always going to do the Power (high catch) versions of the lifts.
So, what is this "S" pull exactly?

Using the **"S"** pull, you drive the bar from the floor, inward toward yourself on a diagonal path through an area called the **Power Zone.** It proceeds to the **Launch Point**, on or near the hips, where you propel it upwards and slightly outwards and then draw it back in towards you at the completion of its journey. The bar's proper pathway loosely resembles a capital "S".

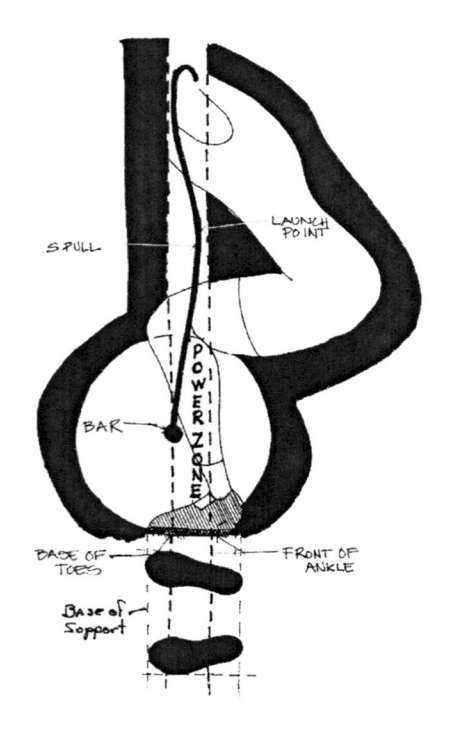

The "S" pull is the best way to pull (drive) a bar from the floor during the Olympic lifts because it allows you to remain centered over your base of support longer, as you try to deliver force to the bar. Using the "S" pull, along with the lower hip starting positions, which is the position used by the best today, your center of mass and the bar will start closer and stay closer during the all phases of the lift. This lower hip position and a more upright back will put you in a stronger position to overcome the inertia of the resting bar on the platform. This position allows you to efficiently use your lats to sweep the bar inward while your knee extensors (quadriceps) work to straighten your legs, driving the bar upward toward your hips. The bar should never go around the knees but, rather, you have to push your knees back out of the way of the bar as it comes toward you.

Further along in the pull, the bar can be more easily controlled because 1) it is moving toward you and 2) you have been able to remain more centered over your base of support in a more stable and flat-footed position. The powerful muscles involved in hip extension have been spared to this point. Your back has actually bowed over slightly here, and will soon be put in an advantageous position for delivering force to the bar using a movement called a <u>double-knee</u> <u>bend</u> (covered in more detail later).

Upon reaching the Launch Point, the bar is <u>catapulted</u> through the next phase of the lift called the 2nd pull. It accelerates quickly <u>upward</u> and slightly away from you. The use of the "S" pull style allows this 2nd phase of the lift to stay closer to you, remaining over your base of support, so you can more easily control and accelerate your movements as you finish your ascent and start your descent to the catch (Power or Full Squat) position.

Summing up, the "S" pull keeps the bar closer to you throughout the task presented by the Olympic-style lifts, allows the hips to take command of the movement, as they should. If this pull is done properly, it allows you to drive the bar more efficiently through the Power Zone and react more efficiently during the last phases of the lift.

<u>Catapulting</u> refers to the technique used by lifters during the 2nd pull of the Olympic lifts. It is characterized by violent hip extension and minimal (if any) loss of contact with the floor. This style is nothing new in the sport of Olympic weightlifting around the world, but simply a term to describe it. <u>Catapulting</u> is substantially different in form and muscle group emphasis from the predominant pulling technique taught in much of the U.S. that advocates propelling the bar upward by employing some kind of jumping or driving motion dominated by a conscious, aggressive knee extension and a conscious triple extension directed at driving the bar higher.

Answer #2: Stay in the "POWER ZONE"

When performing these Olympic-style lifts, the first rule for delivering the most force to the bar with the "S" or any other pull and for performing the quickest gymnastic catching or racking movement around the bar is: KEEP IT CLOSE. You can do a lot of things right and not perform a good Olympic-style lift if you fail to follow this rule.

When you set yourself correctly and start the 1st pull (drive) from the floor, you have to start moving the bar towards yourself as efficiently and directly as proper technique and the limitations of your body type will allow. And, during the 2nd pull, the bar should move upward and not swing away from you out past the front of the feet. I call the imaginary vertical column rising from your base of support and bordered by the front of your ankle and the base of your toes, **The Power Zone**.

All forces that you produce that affect the bar should keep the bar in this Zone. If you do something to the bar that forces it forward of this Zone, it will lead to inefficient technique or missed lifts. Sometimes certain techniques tilt the line of the "S" to the rear with good results, but you must be very aware of what you are doing for this to be useful. Athletes and coaches from sports other than Olympic weightlifting can generally think of this Power Zone as the weightlifting equivalent of "the wheelhouse" or "the groove".

When you pull the bar correctly using the S pull, the deeper towards the middle of the POWER ZONE the bar moves on its diagonal line towards the hips during the 1st pull, the better. This assumes you are staying in correct lifting positions. The more centrally the bar is located in that POWER ZONE when explosive hip extension is initiated at the LAUNCH POINT, the better. The major technical advantage of the "S" pulling style is that it brings the bar to your hips, rather than have your hips chase a bar that is going by somewhere in front of them.

If you employ the older "straight pull", you will still have to keep the bar within this POWER ZONE. Lifters that use this technique often have the bar move outwards right after it leaves the floor, which will make it very difficult to keep it in the middle of this zone and therefore, make it unlikely that the lift will be efficient or fast.

It is possible that the bar will move forward of the Power Zone column slightly after being catapulted from the hips when using the "S" pull or the straight pull. That line of drive can be perfectly fine, but this distance and time near or in front of the Zone should and can be limited. As you get stronger and better technically, the bar will seldom, if ever, be out of the POWER ZONE.

There are variations of the "S" pull by some of the extremely talented Olympic weightlifters, including tilting the entire "*S*" towards the rear of the POWER ZONE and actually jumping backwards into a full squat to rack the bar. This and other techniques have appeared and are used by Olympic weightlifters in the quest of a more efficient method of getting under the massive weights they attempt to lift. For most of you, this is a little too extreme and just gets in the way of what you really need to know and do. For Olympic weightlifters, I will talk about this later in the book and have my lifters demonstrate some of the more exotic variations on the DVD.

The drills I write about below and show you on the DVD are all geared towards teaching you an orthodox "S" pull. It will help you to drive the bar when performing these lifts.

Answer #3: Sweep the Bar

The **Sweep** is a movement of the bar inward toward the lifter, during the 1st pull that occurs as the bar leaves the floor, block or hanging position. It is initiated by the latisimus dorsi of the lifter that tightens or squeezes slightly to move the arms inward towards the rising lifter.

Sweeping the bar

To easily understand what this movement should look-and-feel like, have a friend stand beside you and hold your shoulder in a slightly forward of neutral position. Hang your arm straight by your side with your elbow facing outward. Have your friend put his other hand in the palm of your hand and push your hand forward. Push back against the resistance while keeping your shoulder in the forward of neutral position. The large muscle of the upper back called the latissimus dorsi or lats is moving your arm to the rear and *sweeping* your friends hand with it. In Olympic-style weightlifting, you will sweep the bar inward at the start of the 1st pull in the same manner, with the lats simultaneously contracting.

Aiding this movement will be a shift on your feet from front to back at the moment you start the bar moving. Together, they create a pendulum movement of the bar inward toward you as you rise. In practice, the bar will move diagonally in and up as you drive the bar away from the floor toward the Launch Point, which we will look at next.

Answer #4: Keep the "Launch Point" Close to the Hips

The **Launch Point** is simply the point on your upper thighs or hips with which the bar is in contact when the explosive catapulting motion is initiated at the start of the 2nd pull (drive). It is also the point immediately before the highest rate of acceleration of the bar occurs during Olympic-style lifts. And, continuing the catapult analogy to its logical conclusion, it is the basket from which the projectile is launched. Of course, in the case of Olympic-style lifting, the projectile and the Launch Point are moving at their moment of contact.

Everybody's Launch Point is a bit different, due to arm length, grip width and other physical differences between individuals. It is safe to say, however, that, with either of the major Olympic-style lift groups (Clean/Snatch variations), the closer the Launch Point to your hips (really, the top of the pubic bone), the better. This simply places the bar closer to the fulcrum of the major lever system involved in projecting (catapulting) it upward, making it a more efficient system. When done properly, the "S" Pull and the "double-knee bend" help put the bar at a Launch Point that is closer to your hips, while keeping you centered over your base of support.

Bar near middle of base of support

Due to the closer grip during variations of the Clean, the Launch Point is on the upper thigh for most people. The Snatch variations should be launched from the pubic bone and the bar should only skim across your upper thighs, if it touches them at all. Only those of you who are actually too big for the dimensions of the Olympic bar or those purposely using an overly close grip, have any reason to use a lower Launch Point than this for the Snatch lifts.

There comes a time when you might, in order to get the bar to a higher Launch Point, adjust your grip outward or try some other trick to gain biomechanical advantage during this part of the lift. While expert lifters can experiment with these changes, I suggest that if you make changes, make them small and take your time with any change you make. Changes in positions can help but many times an advantage gained at one point is lost at another.

**Answer #5: Perfect the "Double-Knee Bend"
(The Scoop)**

The advent of the "S" pull, more emphasis on the development of the musculature of the legs and the backsides of athletes, and lower starting positions when performing the Olympic-style lifts put more accent on a movement called *the double-knee bend* or *scoop.* This movement amounts to the repositioning of the hips and back at the end of the 1st pull to more efficiently deliver force in a purposeful direction to the bar as it enters the explosive 2nd pull.

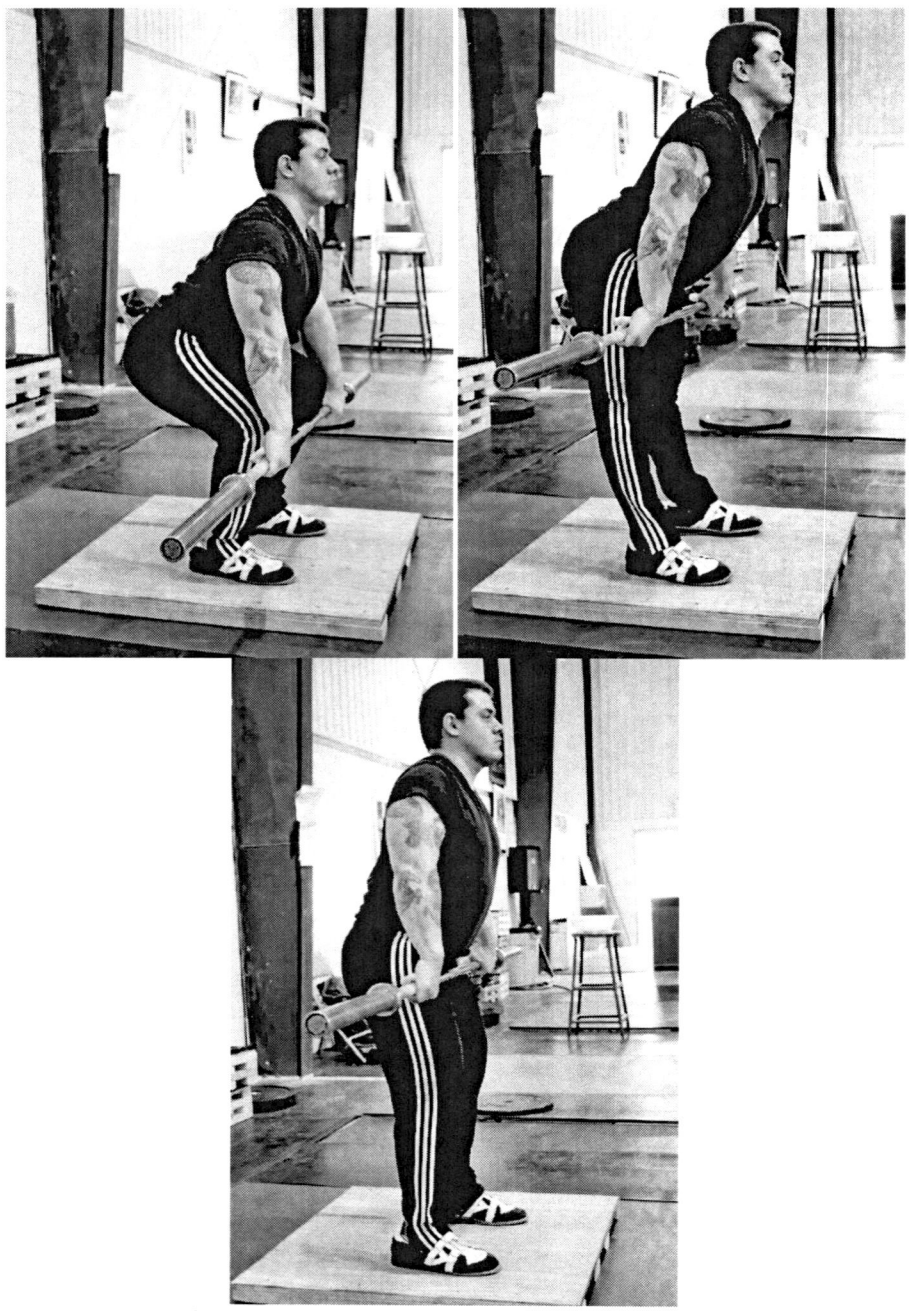

Completing the double-knee bend or scoop

The term double-knee bend alludes to the fact that the knees are bent at first in the Set position and re-bent (allowed to bend) at the end of the 1st pull, before you initiate the 2nd pull. They are <u>scooped</u> back under the bar as it moves upward and inward toward the Launch Point.

As you pull (drive) the bar from the floor by forceful knee extension, it moves upward and inward towards you. Your torso tilts forward here, as well. Just before your knees reach full extension, you <u>allow</u> them to travel forward, while raising your back slightly (the scoop). This results in two advantageous things happening. Your hips are lowered and your back is angled more towards vertical. By using this method you have taken full advantage of your powerful knee extensors to move the bar from the floor toward the hips and have then quickly reset your even more powerful hip extensors in a better position to then deliver an <u>upward</u> blow, or explosive <u>catapulting</u> action to the bar. (This is similar to a high jumper lowering his hips when he takes the gather step just before exploding upward.) In weightlifting, the scoop brings the Launch Point to the still ascending bar and puts you in a balanced position over your base of support to deliver force to it.

This scoop, if possible, should be accomplished without leaving the rear half of your feet. It is crucial that if forceful hip extension is to be maximized, it should be initiated from a flat-footed stance with the balance over the rear half of the feet. Due to the structural differences in humans, this is not always possible, but it is still preferred. (More on the double-knee bend in Chapter V.)

Answer #6: Think of a "Power Circle" when You Lift

Power Circle is a term I have used for many years to describe the rhythm of the Olympic lifts. It is a mental technique to deal with the complications of the Olympic lifts. It is not, by strict definition, correct, but I have always been understood when I explained it to athletes, so I continue to go back to it. I hope it helps you do the lifts better.

Moving through the Power Circle means that when you are doing the Olympic lifts you want to have the feeling that you are moving yourself faster through each successive phase of the lift, until you catch the bar overhead or on your shoulders. I want you to be thinking of this rather than the real change of direction that is occurring. Continual acceleration through a circular pattern is easier for the brain to deal with than all the intricacies of the actual movements. Much more than that overloads the brain during powerful movements.

Power Circle (start to finish)

I know, for instance, that the bar slows when the double knee bend occurs before being re-accelerated in the explosive 2nd pull. I know you will be slower in your assent at this point, no matter how fast you are. I know that power output is less at this point. I know that during the Olympic lifts, you are going up, and then down, then up again and down again, finally reaching the catch position, not really in a circle. And, I know one more thing. Knowing all that is irrelevant when it comes down to actually doing an Olympic lift.

I want you to keep trying to make your body go faster as you go through the lift. You should never feel as though there is any slowing down or lessening of your effort during the lift, until you have the bar on your shoulders or overhead. This is how you produce athletic power: Slower to faster until it's done. If a movement slows in the middle, do that part of it as quickly as possible. If it changes direction completely, don't stall. Make the change as fast as you can.

Answer #7: Separate the unorthodox from the just plain wrong.

There are not one thousand ways to skin a cat. There are five or six that work. The rest just give you a chopped up cat. (I'm a cat owner; so don't send me nasty letters about this.) Basically, this means you've got to separate the variations that might occur in techniques because of body-type from techniques that have no basis in scientific fact whatsoever. The

basic things that can be said about proper form in the 1ˢᵗ pull, for instance, are that the shoulders of lifters should be vertically (or nearly) over the bar, arms should travel downward by the sides of the knees of the lifters, lifters hips should be lower rather than higher and their balance should be over the rear half of their feet though most of this phase of the lift.
There are more positional variations that are acceptable that occur during the rest of the phases that may be acceptable. Later in this book you'll read what I suggest. But, here, I will offer a bit of advice to both lifters and coaches.

Don't make or accept adjustments in the basic, proper positions for weightlifting that attempt to make up for every individual's deficits in strength or flexibility. Make these individuals stronger and more flexible so they can attain and maintain the basic, proper positions for weightlifting.

This, of course, isn't actually a technique of lifting but one of thinking about it like any other physical skill. If, for instance, you can't keep your left arm straight during a golf swing, you don't buy into somebody saying you should bend it as much as you can and straighten in when you hit the ball. You work on flexibility and work on recognizing your limitations in the swing. That's because you know there aren't a thousand ways to hit a golf ball well. There are minor variations that work, but beyond that you're just wasting your time. Same with weightlifting.

*****

More about Getting to the Launch Point

Concerning the bar and its journey to the Launch Point during proper Olympic-style lifting, there are two pretty simple rules you must know.

1. When lifted from any point below the Launch Point, the bar should continually move diagonally toward you until it reaches the Launch Point.
2. As the bar nears the Launch Point, the double-knee bend occurs, moving your Launch Point downward and forward to meet the bar.

IMPORTANT

I have observed that this initial diagonal movement is not used by many weightlifters when they are working from the hang or from blocks. The usual (and wrong) technique used is to simply set your shoulders somewhere out over the bar, drive upward from whatever block the bar happens to be set on or the height at which it is hanging. This leads to reinforcing a pull line that is incorrect, and bad technique from the floor is bound to follow.

The correct way to do the Olympic-style lifts from blocks or the hang is to first put your shoulders and the bar in the same relationship that they would have if you were in the Set position down on the platform. Your shoulders should be vertically over the bar, and your balance on the rear of your feet, whether the bar is on a block or hanging, as long as it is below the Launch Point. To pull correctly from either, you should initially make a strong effort to sweep the bar inward and move your knees to the rear, just as would be happening in a good pull from the floor.

Start all these from the same shoulder to bar relationship

And sweep in before the scoop

You should then continue the lift as you would if it had come from the floor by performing a double-knee bend, causing the meeting of the bar and the Launch Point. At that point you initiate the explosive 2nd pull and the bar is driven upward. This positioning and movement applies whether it is going to be a complete lift, ending in a full squat or a high (Power) catch position or if it is simply a Pull.

By doing Block or Hang lifts in this manner, you will constantly reinforce the correct "S" pull line, muscle use sequence and double-knee bend that you should be using from the floor. After a short time, you will find this pull line natural from all positions.

CHAPTER II: PPaDftT-SM
Preparatory Positions and Drills for the Ten-Step Method

The drills, positions and techniques covered in this chapter will be covered in detail in the DVD. I suggest that you watch the DVD as you read through this chapter. A lot of the basics are covered here and it will help you to see and hear, as well as read these explanations.

How Can I Learn Proper Technique?

I am going to show you a new method of learning proper technique. Why? There are several methods used by national organizations to teach the Olympic-style lifts. There are many others employed by coaches around the country. The following are my reasons for presenting a different method of teaching the lifts.

I have a big problem with the way Olympic-style lifts are taught in this country. The problem is threefold. The first problem is that many coaches in this country seem to assume when they start teaching you these Olympic-style lifts, that you already have a sufficient amount of body and spatial awareness and that you possess the particular physical strength needed to correctly perform these movements.

Even among the athletes that have participated in sports such as football, basketball and soccer from an early age, one or more of these qualities are either missing or minimal. That doesn't mean that you aren't strong, agile or don't possess any spatial awareness. It means that you don't have the correct balance of all these gifts to perform the Olympic-style lifts efficiently, and in all likelihood you haven't practiced the whole range of skills you need to do these odd and very important lifts.

The second problem is that the overall technique that many coaches are trying to teach to is obsolete, inefficient or simply wrong. A great many programs taught by certified coaches from national weightlifting organizations have disseminated these techniques and continue to do so. They have been passed along from other coaches who also learned faulty or simply older techniques. Therefore, I am not at all surprised that technique used in Olympic-style lifting by many of you in the lower grades, high school, as well as in many college programs, bears little resemblance to the techniques used throughout the rest of the world today by international level weightlifters and other athletes who have learned under those systems. And, for the same reason, I am also not surprised that the sport of Olympic Weightlifting in this country has not been successful internationally for many years.

The <u>third problem</u> is that the progressions that many use to teach the Olympic-style lifts are complicated or counter-productive. The design is without foundation or logic. They are based on faulty assumptions about the nature of modern weightlifting, and misinterpretations of techniques now used worldwide.

To address the first problem, I will present a method of learning the Olympic lifts that includes preparatory drills for you to practice before you ever try to do the lifts. They will get you thinking correctly about how your body will have to operate when you do these lifts. These drills will not take the place of the correct physical training (play) that all of you should have had throughout your childhood, but it will provide enough to get most of you started on the right path in achieving fairly good technique in and gaining the benefits of the Olympic-style lifts.

Many correct movements in Olympic-style lifting don't seem to make any common sense. That doesn't mean they're wrong. That simply means that your brains haven't been taught that these movements will accomplish the overall task better. The drills below should start to help you learn the body positions and balance for better Olympic-style weightlifting.

The sports that most of you have played involve lots of forward and side-to-side and vertical movement and an emphasis on the muscles that move you forward, forward and laterally or forward and upwards in succession. Even when you are moving backwards in sports, you are doing so while balanced over the balls of your feet. The movements involved in correctly performing the Olympic-style lifts demand that you think differently about how to move. I will provide a few basic drills that will allow you to reorient yourself quickly to the direction needed when performing Olympic-style lifts, as well as the balance points and muscles that need to be emphasized to attain the best results.

As far as the second problem of overall technique, I will gear these teaching steps to guide you towards the latest technique of Olympic-style lifting used in the world. I think it is sensible to copy the best technique used by athletes who lift the most weight using these lifts. I do not vary the basic technique for those of you competing in sports outside the sport of Olympic Weightlifting. All of you should be learning correct technique in these lifts as ardently as you learn the best and latest techniques in the performance of your own sports.

Regarding the third problem, I have created a fairly simple and logical method of teaching all of you good technique when performing the Olympic lifts. This methods concentrates on teaching you how to make hip extension more dominant, natural and rhythmic, and will teach you how to properly drive from and with the hips (glutes) when performing these lifts.

Gas Station Break

COACHES: Too often in this country coaches try to "excite" their athletes about lifting by getting right to the Olympic-style lifts and ignore the basic skills needed for having an athlete properly prepared to do these lifts. To me this approach is like trying to teach a basketball player the intricacies of the 2-1-2-zone defense before teaching him to dribble properly or even what the basketball feels like.

I have seen, time and time again, the damage produced by this type of "short cut" approach. In the long run, it not only damages you but it damages the perceived value of these lifts.

Coach John Wooden, arguably the greatest basketball coach of all time, used to start each year's first practice session by talking to his highly touted recruits and veteran players about how to properly put their socks on! Imagine how tedious that was to these "cream of the crop" players.

What follows will help you all put your "weightlifting socks" on first. If you lose interest, that's your tough luck. I'd rather produce one athlete that knows exactly what he is doing and why than a hundred with sloppy technique and no clue about how to perform the Olympic-style lifts.

*****

(To Parents)

You're going to start feeling a bit left out from here on in, but you should read on to get a general idea of what a coach should be teaching your son or daughter about weightlifting and what your child is spending so much time in front of that mirror and doing a lot of other things that might seem odd. Fact is though; the coach/athlete relationship will be primary during the training sessions. And, that is how it should be.

*****

Here's Where You Start to Learn Technique.

The Warm up

When you first get to the gym, do a good fifteen-minute dynamic (moving around) warm-up. As you warm up, the coach can look at possible deficiencies that you might have to concentrate a bit more on them later. For instance, if you can't do a simple grapevine, you are probably going to need some work on rhythm, agility and hip flexibility. Start dealing with it soon.
My preferred warm-up is usually 2 x 10 meters of each of the following:

1. Walking high knee hugs
2. Skipping knee-ups
3. Walking medium-hi kicks
4. Jogging butt kicks
5. Walking arm swings
6. Walking arm circles
7. Forward lunge walking
8. Side step, up and over squat walking
9. Grape vines (left and right side leads)
10. Burpees (~10 in place)
11. Snatch grip overhead squats w/PVC dowel or light bar (10 repetitions)

Now, you might differ a bit on what you do in a warm-up but whatever exercises you prefer, try to get the quads, posterior chain, torso and shoulder muscles warm and get your heart rate up a bit. If you break a sweat, that's nice. You'll be ready to do some work. You might even jog around a bit, if you want…unless you're a weightlifter or a discus, hammer thrower because all weightlifters and throwers believe that--------**"Running breeds cowardice."** That's their story, and they're sticking to it. (Actually, that's just their feeble rationalization for trying to get out of any running whatsoever.)

Those of you who are larger athletes should start the warm-up with a 5-minute ride on a stationary bike or, better yet, a rower (Concept II is the best). Skipping rope can always be included for those of you who are good at it (and, all athletes should get good at it). A bit of abdominal and back work is okay at the completion of the basic warm-up drills above.

Now, let's start the basic drills.

Just Standing Around Looking in a Mirror
(Whose that Handsome Devil?)

Now, you're not bodybuilders or pathological narcissists (Is that redundant?) but a full length mirror can come in handy in learning what "straight back," "bodyweight on the heels," "below parallel," "drive vertically through the heels," mean. The mirror can come in handy for the more veteran athletes to recheck form as well. Just don't carry it around with you. People will talk.

*****

Gas Station

COACHES: Demonstrate the positions or lifts you want the athlete to perform prior to having him attempt it. Try to do this as often as possible as it will build confidence in the athlete as to your ability and we can never underestimate the sense of sight as a teaching channel. If you physically can't do a movement, get an assistant who can to demonstrate it for the athletes.

I'll add one more thing here. Skip these drills and lifts at your peril. I don't care if they seem simple and boring. These are basic concepts that are necessary for proper lifting and you will not be familiar with one or more of them. That will hinder your athletes' overall progress and how closely you can come to getting the most out of your weightlifting program. And, that may keep you from reaching your athletes' potential. They already have "holes". Don't dig more.

You can do the following drills without a mirror but I will guarantee they will pick up better positional habits faster if you have athletes use one from the start as an assisting prop.

Corrections will be easier to make if they can look and see while you adjust them to the correct positions.

Throughout the following lessons, verbally express what you want your athlete to do, while you demonstrate it yourself or help your athlete through these positions or lifts. SILENCE IS STUPID.

Drill #1: Front, Back and Middle of the Foot Drill

Stand in front of the mirror (left or right side to mirror) with your heels just wider than your hips and toes pointed forward. Arms should be hanging down normally. Knees should stay comfortably straight during this lesson.

1. Stand straight, while being sideways to a full-length mirror.
2. Move to your heels without causing the front of your feet to rise from the floor.
3. Hold that position for about five to ten seconds. ("on the heels")
4. Move back to mid-foot and hold position for the same duration of time. ("in the middle")
5. Now, move to the balls of your feet without causing your heels to rise from the floor. ("on the front")
6. Again, hold this position for five to ten seconds.
7. Stand straight and sway to the same three positions, holding each particular one for the same duration of time as above and watching yourself in the mirror as you do it.
8. Repeat these three positions until you are as comfortable on the heels as the balls of your feet.

This drill can be used as a normal part of warming up as long as you need it. Although it seems simple, many of you aren't really aware of where your heels are or how to balance through them and that will be incredibly important in weightlifting and other sport activities as well.

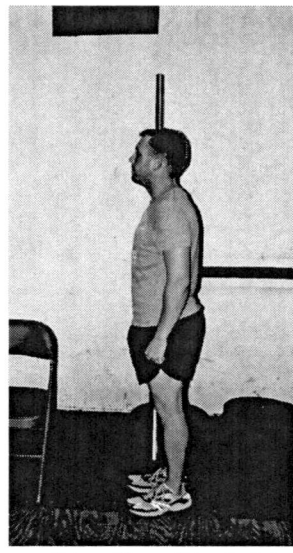

Standing Straight 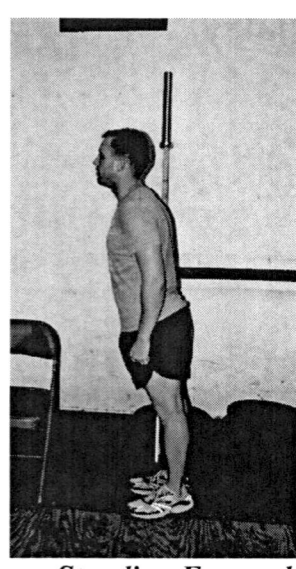   *Standing Forward* 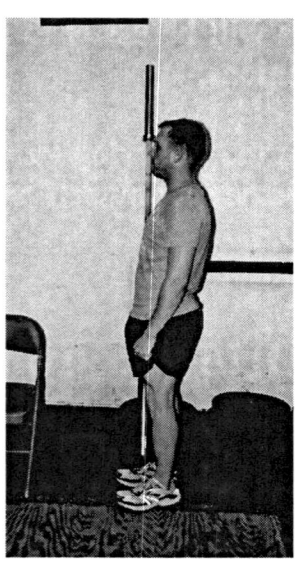   *Standing Back*

Drill #2: The Straight/Angled Back

When performing the Olympic-style lifts, or most weightlifting movements, the back has to be straight. Now, what is that exactly and how do you achieve it? In Olympic-style lifting when we refer to a "straight back" it is one that is only slightly arched and probably tilted forward at some angle.

Straight/Angled Back

This can be a very difficult thing to learn when you are new to lifting. The tendency is for coaches to put a bar in front of you and tell you to get down and grab it and keep your back straight or arched or flat and stick your tailbone (or butt) out, up or back. What follows, more often than not, is that you bend over and your spine ends up looking like a camel's hump or a scared cat on a picket fence. Funny: Yes. Useful: No.

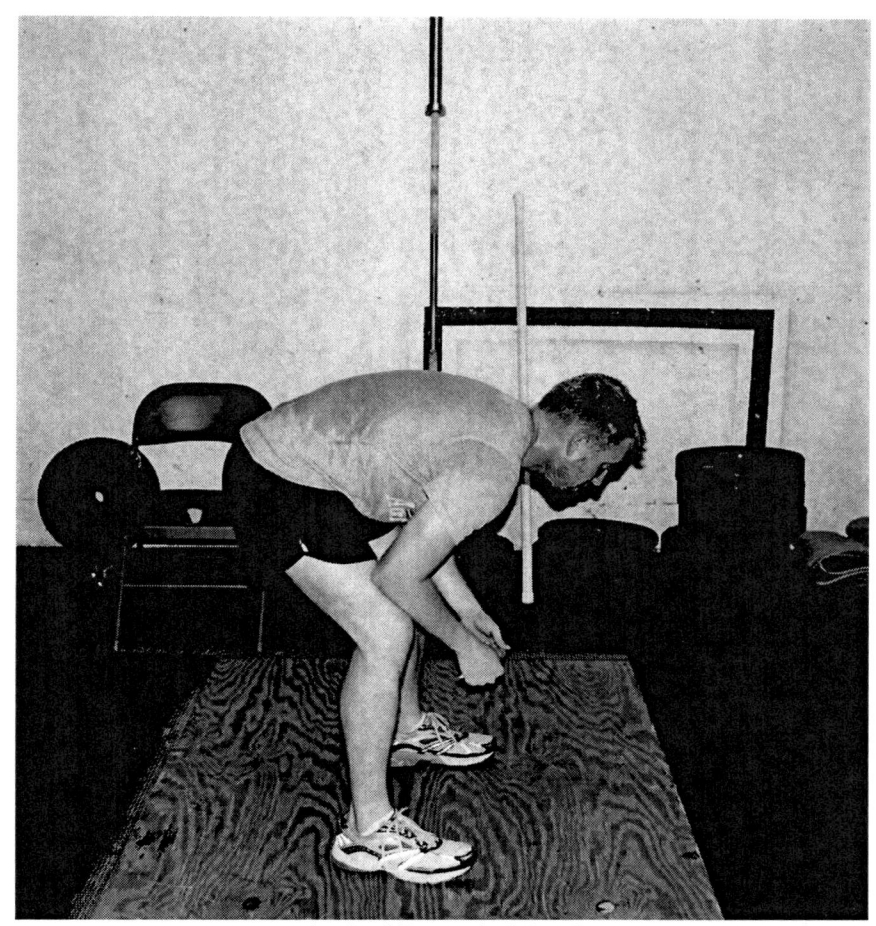

Arched/Rounded Back

*****

A much better method to use to teach this concept is to, once again, go to the mirror. This time, bring along a four to five foot piece of PVC pipe or a broomstick.

1. Stand sideways to the mirror and squat down slightly, with your forearms resting on your thighs.
2. Have a buddy lay the stick along your back and keep your upper back and tailbone touching the bar, while your lower back is just out of contact with it.

You can look at this while you are doing it and a coach or friend can tap his fingers on your lower back to cue you sure if it starts to round and touch the stick. You now have accomplished a position that can be very frustrating if you try learning it differently: the angled, straight back.

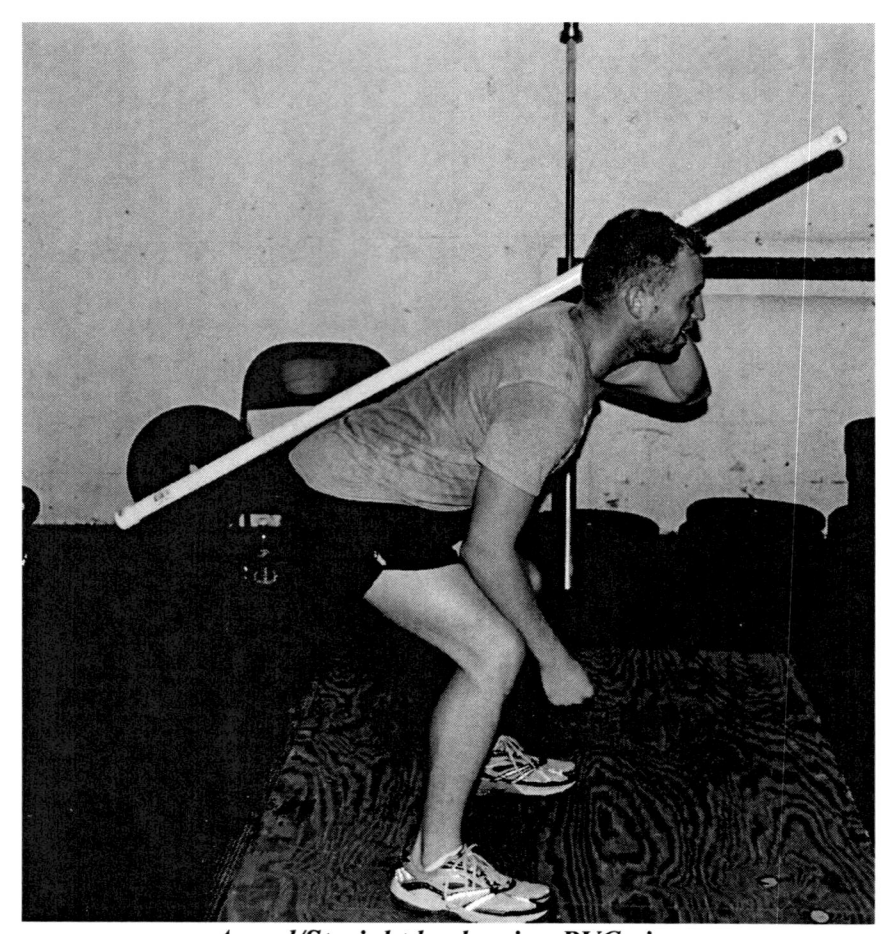

Anged/Straight back using PVC pipe

You may find that you can use this PVC pipe to achieve a straight, angled back when you put a bar on the floor, in front of you to do the fine tuning on your Set position (starting position).

Drill #3: The Heel Jump
(Discovering what hip extension really is and where it starts.)

Learn to jump with only your heels touching the floor. I know it's not a good way to jump. That's not what I'm trying to teach you here. I want you to start to be aware of the posterior chain (back, butt, hamstrings especially), as well as how and where to initiate hip extension in the <u>explosive</u> <u>catapulting</u> of the bar in the 2nd pull when you're performing the Olympic-style lifts.

Here it is, step by step:

1. Move to the front of a raised platform (it should be no more than an inch or so off the floor) and hang the front of your feet off, keeping them in mid-air, parallel to the floor.
2. Extend your arms to the front, keeping them parallel to the floor, for balance.
3. Bend your knees and tilt your torso slightly forward into a jumping position.
4. Jump, without letting the front of your feet touch the floor and without swinging your arms.
5. When you land back on the platform, land on your heels, knees bent and arms forward, ready to jump again.
6. Do this 10-20 times in succession, if you can. Then try it with your hands clasped behind your neck.

Heel Jump-hip extension/flexion

This drill uses an unnatural position to teach you that you can produce force through hip extension without being on the front of your feet, which is a much more natural sports position. I want you to start learning to think from and about the hips (or butt, if you wish). That's the body's muscle center and that's where power lives. Use it well and you will have an advantage over most other athletes, no matter what the sport. The heels are where, ideally, the explosive 2nd pull or "catapulting" of the Olympic-style lifts begins. Remember that.

Please don't misunderstand. The front of the feet and the quads (front thigh muscles) will become involved in the actual movement, but not to the extent they get involved when an athlete is, say, jumping or running. The big job for the quadriceps at this point will be to move your feet to the proper catch positioning. They have already performed their primary function in driving the bar during the 1st pull. The muscles of the posterior chain (back, glutes, hamstrings, calves) are in the driver's seat when it comes to Olympic-style lifts and, in fact, initiate many efficient, full-body power movements. You have to become more aware of the muscles involved in these BIG movements if you expect to lift big weights, or simply play your sport with more power, and this drill will begin to help you do that.

Drill #4: Dirty Dancing

There are about one thousand jokes about this drill and I've heard them all. In fact, I've told most of them. This, joking aside, is one of the most important prerequisite drills to learning how to correctly accelerate a bar in the 2nd pull. Basically, it teaches you to stay on the floor, hip-extend and then hip-flex rapidly back to the original position. This mimics the actions, direction and timing of the 2nd pull and the entrance to the 3rd pull (Pull-under).

It reminds me of a dance move but its intent is to get you to deliver a blow with your hips quickly and retract them quickly. Think of it as throwing a jab and bringing your fist back to defensive position. This teaches you to extend your hips and then descend quickly, just as they will do in the real lifts.

This is done without a bar. <u>Make sure your heels never leave the floor, unless drawn slightly off by the force of the hip extension.</u> No triple extension here.

1. Stand flat-footed with your feet about shoulder width apart and your arms out a bit for balance.
2. Flex your knees and your hips about so that you descend to about the position you would be in at the beginning of the 2nd pull.
3. Your balance should be over your heels at this point.
4. Quickly extend your hips <u>upward</u> fully and extend your knees to a point just before full knee extension. (your balance will travel forward in your feet and there will be some forward movement of your hips)

5. Quickly flex your hips and return to the original position with the balance over the heels again.
6. Do this ten times in ten seconds, if you can. Then, do three to four sets of this.

Dirty Dancing-hip extension/flexion

This drill teaches you how to fire your hips (glutes) through full extension and regain position quickly. This is what the hips have to do when <u>catapulting</u> a bar <u>upward</u> and then start descending to a receiving position. If you can't do this drill, you need to work on your rhythm and agility at the hips. That is essential for efficient Olympic-style weightlifting. Remember, Olympic weightlifting requires that you teach the gross motor muscles to be as agile as fine motor muscles. Work this last drill until it's natural.

Drill #5: Now, Up Against the Wall.

The **Jerk** is a powerful movement in which a bar is driven from your shoulders overhead to arms length in a continuous motion. It is essential to good Olympic-style weightlifting and an important training lift for many sports. It begins with a lowering of your hips, accomplished by allowing the knees to move forward and finishes with an explosive vertical hip and leg drive and a quick, punching lockout of the arms without hesitation or slowing, immediately following this.

This is the initial drill I use to teach athletes the Jerk dip and drive sequence. This will also apply to the start of the Push Press dip and drive, except I advise that the dip be a bit longer for that lift than the one for the Jerk. This is pretty simple and requires very little in the way of equipment except a flat wall.

1. Stand straight, feet angled just slightly outward and back to the wall, with your heels two to four inches away from the wall.
2. Put your arms horizontally in front of you.
3. Keep your glutes and shoulders against the wall throughout this exercise.
4. Allow your knees to go forward and dip down through his heels for three to six inches. Then drive back up through the heels until you are standing straight. This should all be done flat-footed.
5. The tempo of this should be slow down fast up with no stopping. Do three sets of 10 reps.
6. Eventually, drive up fast enough that the hip extension lifts you onto the balls of your feet. (In the completed drive, you will push off to the catch position through the balls of your feet.)
7. Repeat this drill until it is reasonably normal for you to start the Jerk drive through your heels and not transfer to the forefeet too early on the upward drive.

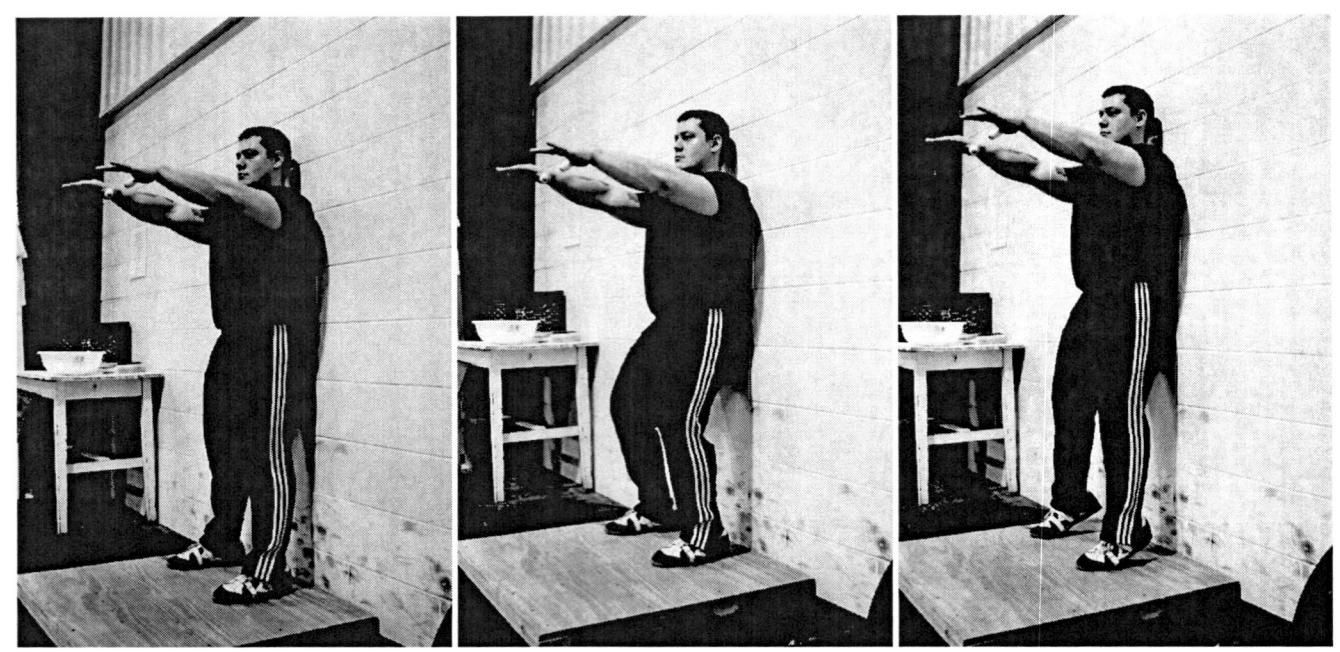

Dip and Drive against wall

This is an important drill because it will help rid you of a whole lot of prior learning. Almost any time in the past that you have dipped down playing sports, you have jumped up. And that meant tilting your torso forward slightly while dipping down and driving upwards through the front of your feet. That will not work for the Jerk. Because the bar is already in front of you (and heavy), that movement will drive the bar forward, where it can't be controlled overhead. It will also get your shoulder and arm muscles involved much too early in the drive, which will probably leave the bar short of arm's length, which is required for a true Jerk. The push through the front of the feet comes in very late in the drive sequence when performing the Jerk.

The bar driveline in a good jerk travels vertically downwards during the dip and slightly diagonally up and toward the rear as you drive it overhead. Odd, huh. But that's what happens if things go right. I'll go into greater depth about the driveline later in this book. Right now, drill that dip and drive through the heels.

*Some of you will Jerk perfectly fine with your feet straight forward. Many will be better served by having a slight outward angle to their feet. The knees should always follow the line of the feet in any driving sequence in Olympic-style lifting. If that rule is followed, this slight outward angle can help deliver force better for many and help prevent buckling of the knees inward during the dip.

Those are the basic drills or, more correctly, preparatory drills that will start you thinking correctly about the basic positions, balance and movements needed to perform these lifts. Now, let's talk about you and the Olympic bar.

How Should I hold the Bar?

**The Clean Grip Width
(Power Clean too)**

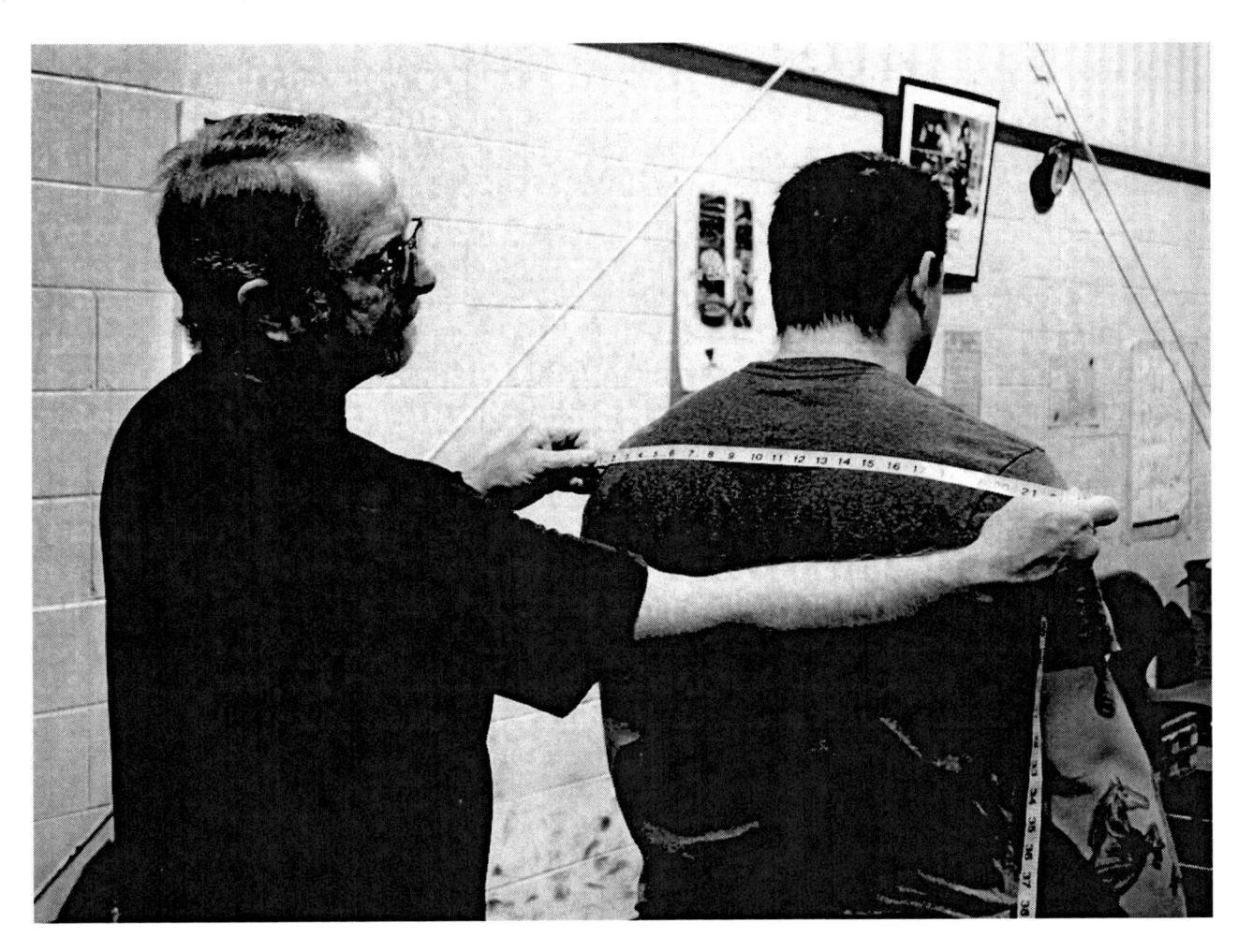

The first grip we will talk about is the one you will need at the **"Set position"** (starting position of Olympic-style lifts at the floor level) for performing the Clean or Power Clean pictured earlier. You will maintain this grip width through the racking of the bar on your shoulders. Have someone measure your shoulders across the back. Use that measurement as the distance between the insides of your hands when you place them on the bar. <u>Be sure to center yourself on the bar first</u>. I generally use this as the initial grip placement. It prevents the hands from being caught between the bar and your shoulders when you first rack (catch) the bar on your collarbones during a Clean or Power Clean. This grip also usually ensures that the lifter will be able to fit his shoulders between the hands during the overhead lifts, such as the Military Press, the Push Press and the Jerk.

If you don't happen to have a measuring tape handy, a quick temporary method I use with athletes to set their hands a thumb length from the start of the inside borders of the knurling on the bar for their initial Clean grip. This will work with most average size folks but not small women or children or really big guys. It's good in a pinch, though.

Some athletes use a wider than suggested grip. To a point, a wider grip than normal during any Olympic-style lift will help you catapult the bar more efficiently in the 2nd pull because by essentially shortening your hanging arm length, you make possible for the Launch Point to be nearer the hips. However, when you "shorten" the arm length by widening the grip there are considerations of flexibility, grip on the bar, shoulder stability in the receiving position and back strength through the pull, to consider. Once you've measured your grip distance and you're satisfied with it, don't change it on a whim and if you do change it, do it little by little over a considerable time and allow the body to adapt. This is not something you should do as a newcomer, but after considerable training-time has passed. Even then, keep in mind that at some point gaining one technical advantage can mean losing another.

Another point about the Clean grip that I'll mention here is that some lifters change the Clean grip to a wider grip before they Jerk or Press the weight overhead. This shortens the distance overhead the bar travels to be at a locked position. The wider grip also can help you put your elbows in a lower position prior to the Jerk or the Press and puts the bar in your palms, both of which are advantageous. It can also make it easier for some of you to get your shoulders "through the door"(positioning the shoulders properly under the bar) when jerking or pressing the bar overhead. It works very well for some.

**Snatch Grip
(Power Snatch too)**

This is how to gauge the grip width that you will use for the Snatch/Power Snatch. This grip width does not change during the lift. Centering yourself on the bar, grip the bar and stand with it so it crosses the front of your hips. If the bar is much below or above the pubic bone, adjust the grip until the bar rests across it. That's the grip you want. Have someone measure the distance between the insides of your hands. That will be your correct snatch grip width.

*****

COACHES: Some coaches start young lifters with a grip that's a little closer than this method suggests. This is to make things a little more stable above the head for these lifters until they've gotten a bit stronger in that position. They can be weaned from this as they progress with technique and become stronger. That is a viable variation. I believe it's better to use the orthodox method of setting their hands and staying lighter with the weights for a little longer time to allow adaptation.

Olympic weightlifters who will be doing the full squat or split Snatch competitively may widen their grip further, over time, to get the advantage of getting a better position at the hip or lessening the height the bar needs to be for the lifter to fit under it in good receiving position. Refer to the information I mentioned above about changes in grip. This should only be considered for veteran Olympic weightlifters.
Here are some basics things coaches should do when recording grip width.

1. For consistency, measure the snatch grip from the outside collars of a standard Olympic bar rather than by where the smooth ring-like breaks in the rough knurling are placed. There is no official distance those rings are placed on different makes of bars but the distance between the collars will be the same. At least it's supposed to be.
2. Always have a cloth tape measure with you to make sure of grip distances.
3. Write down these grip distances and keep them with you at all times because inevitably, when your athletes are new at it, they will forget what their grip width is at the worst times.

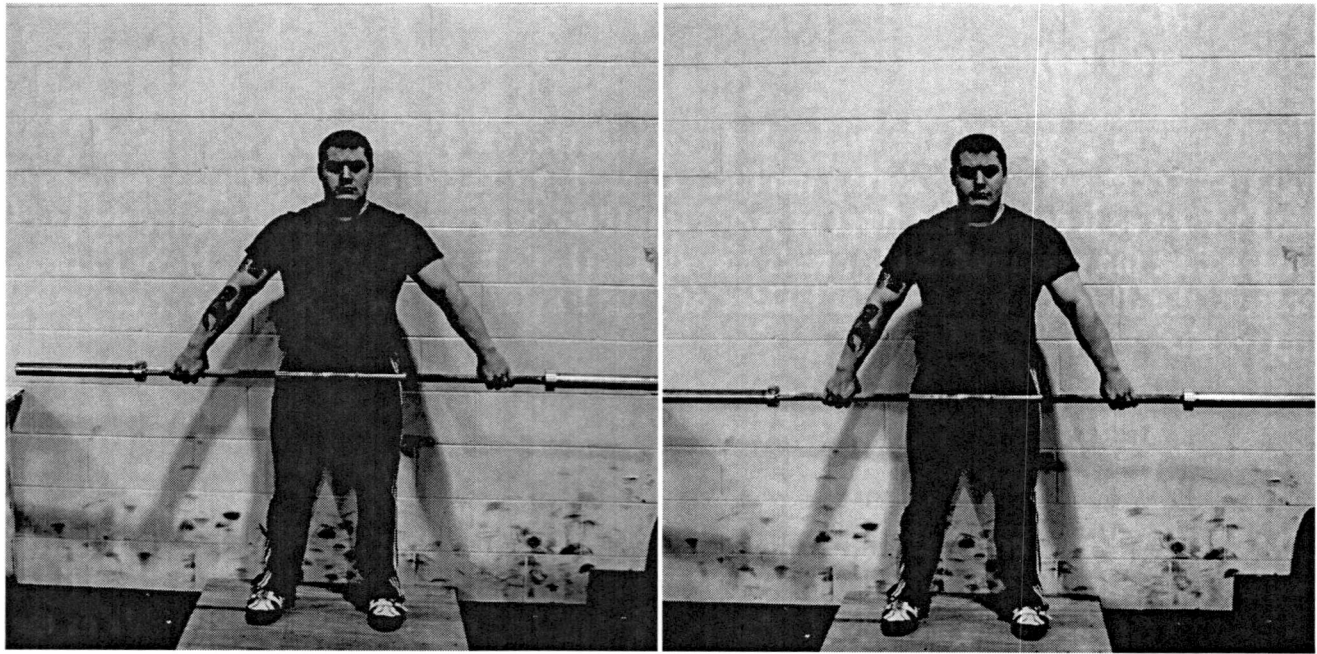

Proper Snatch Grip Width *Improper Snatch Grip Width*

Where Do I Put My Feet at the Set Position?
(How Wide and How Far Under?)

For young children under four feet in height and new to weight lifting, a bar or dowel elevated on blocks to about five inches above the floor is appropriate to learn these positions. For all others, an olympic bar or dowel elevated to the height of loaded, full size bumper (rubber) plates should be used. That's about 8½ inches at the bar's center.

Close
(acceptable)

Standard
(acceptable)

Wide
(acceptable)

Foot placement has gone through some changes over the years. For simplicity, you should place your feet slightly closer than shoulder width with the feet angled out slightly. Both narrower and wider stances (about hip width) are also successfully used by a good number of lifters.

Of a more critical nature is the foot placement under the bar. When standing over the loaded bar and looking down, it should be over the base of your big toe. If you are looking down at your shoes, the bar should be just past the lowest lace holes of your shoes. This positioning is critical for proper use of the more efficient "S" pull, when you are lifting the bar during the Olympic-style lifts.

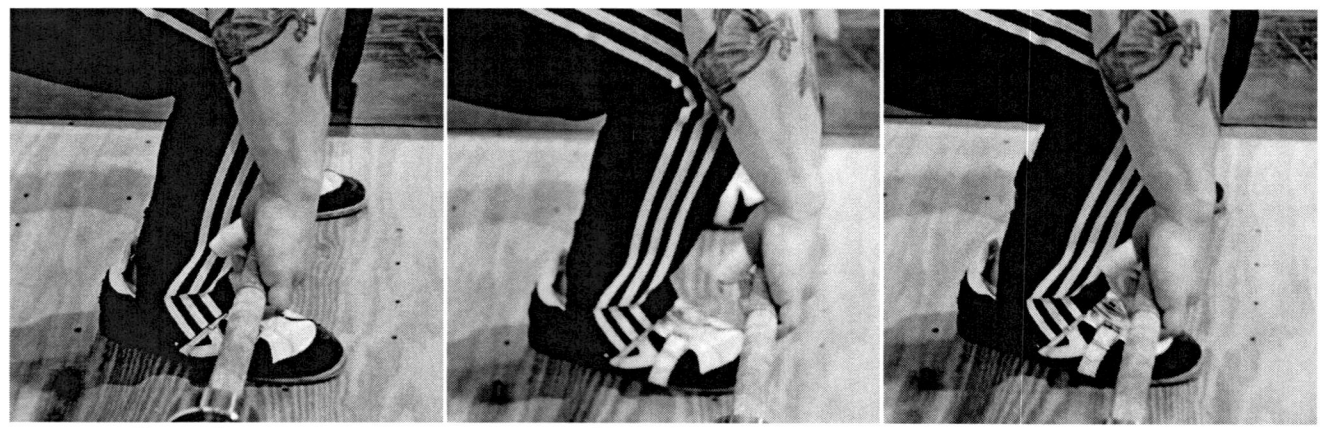

Too close   *Too far*   *Just right*

The balance on your feet is also critical at the Set (starting) position. For most styles of pulling, the balance at the Set position must be on the front of your feet. However, this DOES NOT mean that the heels of the feet should be off the floor. It is a subtle shift within the shoe.

Note to Coaches: There is also a new, unusual technique in which Olympic weightlifters balance over their heels at this point. When using this technique, the bar is slightly closer at the Set position.

*****

The Set Position
(feet, back, shoulders, hips, arms, hands and the bar...WHEW!)

The **Set Position** is the starting position for driving (pulling) the bar from the floor when performing an Olympic-style lift. Try learning the **Set** position using the Clean grip. This grip should keep you more comfortable when initially learning how to correctly position yourself on a bar from the floor. The rules for the Snatch grip Set position are essentially the same as below, except, of course for the hand positions.

1. Hips low. (slightly below or above knee height)
2. Arms straight and descending by the outsides of the knee joints to reach the bar.

3. Feet slightly closer than shoulder width and pointed slightly outwards.
4. Knees always in line with foot direction.
5. Back angled forward and kept straight. (chest facing more forward than down)
6. Knuckles facing down and the bar is hook gripped in Clean or Snatch positions.
7. Shoulders vertically above the bar.
8. The bar placed vertically above the base of the big toe.
9. Bodyweight balanced slightly on the forefeet but heels are on the floor.
10. Elbows pointing towards their respective ends of the bar.
11. Shoulders slightly forward of neutral position, down and relaxed.
12. Traps stretched slightly and lats slightly flared.
13. Head relaxed: in line with torso or facing slightly forward.
14. Eyes forward.

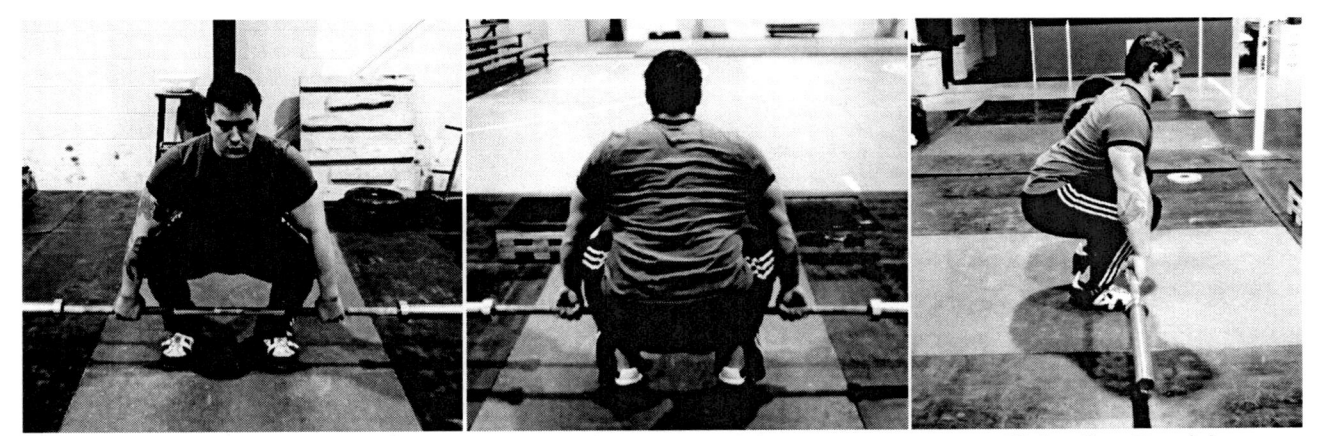

Front-Set Position　　***Back-Set Position***　　***Side-Set Position***

This exact position may not be able to be attainable by everyone at first. Taller athletes and those with weak glutes, hamstrings or those of you lacking a certain degree of flexibility may not be able to lower yourselves to the position seen in the pictures, but taller people can get pretty close to this position when properly taught. Also, torso and/or thigh length may be such that in a good set position, your shoulders are still slightly in front of the bar. This is simply why some people are not as good as others at doing these lifts. No biggie. Keep your shoulders as close to vertical over the bar as you can, given the limitations of your body lengths and work on getting to the positions described above. These Olympic-style lifts will be of tremendous benefit to you, whether you are the perfect weightlifting build or not.

COACH'S NOTE: I always feel as though I'm arching my back when I go to the Set position. This may be a good cue for your athletes, although you actually want them to have a straight back at that position.)

Elbows and Shoulders and Hands
(Oh, my!)

I like to use a 5 ½ to 6-foot long wooden dowel (or PVC) to teach the next few positions. I feel it takes the weight of an actual steel bar out of the picture and allows you to learn more easily. Start by marking your dowels are at the center point, the inside starting points of the knurling, the rings (international) and the inside of the collars of an Olympic bar. This will allow you to become used to what is standard on an Olympic bar and what the terminology is when talking about one. Jargon can stand in the way of learning so the more you use the terms, the easier it'll come.

Hands
The (Dreaded) Hook Grip

This method of gripping the bar should be used for all Olympic style lifts. It hurts. Skin is tough, and it grows back. I haven't seen anyone's thumbs actually fall off yet from employing this gripping method. Start using it right from the beginning with the dowel, and the pain will be minimized, although it will still be a source of laughter for your coaches over the years. And, they need that because the pay is lousy.

When you set your hands for a clean or snatch (or variation) wrap them around the bar at the appropriate distance apart, placing your thumbs underneath the fingers of the respective hand, trapping them against the bar. This grip helps ensure that the bar won't escape from your hands at the start of the lift or at the explosive hip thrust at the start the 2nd pull or anywhere else during its ascent.

Hook Grip   *Fist aimed down*

It is important that the fist created when gripping the bar should be pointed directly down towards the floor. You don't want any bend the wrist at the start of the pull from the floor because it will jar you as you put force through the floor to lift the bar. The arms and hands should seem like a straight rope attaching you to the bar. The muscles of the arms should be relaxed.

You should release the thumbs from the hook when you rack (catch) the bar on your shoulders during the clean or power clean. This becomes an unconscious movement after time. The hook grip is <u>not kept in place</u> during the Jerk or any overhead press. Most lifters keep the hook in during the snatch or variations.

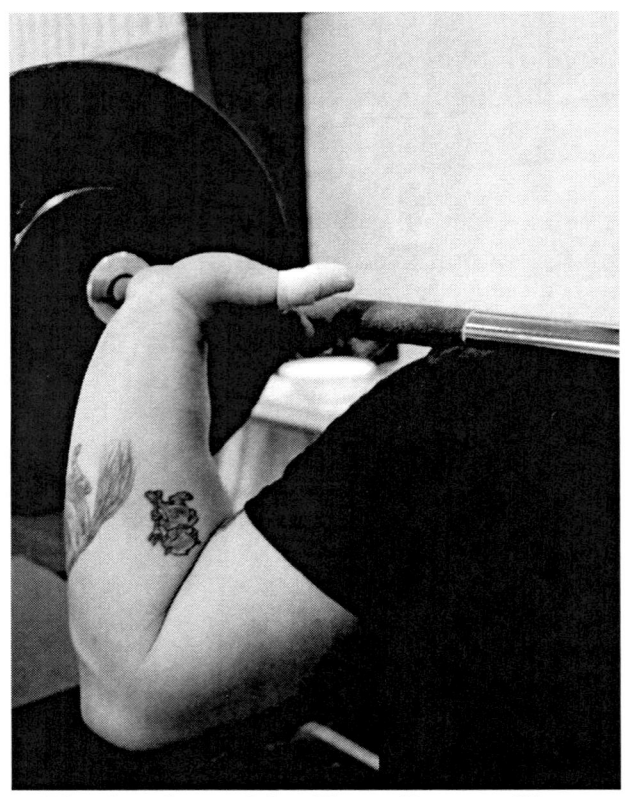

Hook released in Clean/Power Clean

As you release the hook in the receiving position (rack) for the clean or power clean, you may open your hands completely, allowing the bar to move to your fingertips. This allows you to raise your elbows higher, which helps stabilize the bar on your shoulders in the proper position, just behind the front deltoids and across the collarbones. This open hand position is great for the clean but must be altered before the Jerk is attempted. (You may be flexible enough at the wrist that you don't have to do this.)

When attempting to Jerk, Military Press or Push Press, <u>the bar must be placed somewhere in the palms of the hands</u>. If you have moved to the fingertip grip during the Clean, you must make sure the bar gets back into the palms of the hands before the attempted overhead movement. It is very inefficient to Jerk from the fingertip grip.

Bar in the palm for Jerk
--Note lower elbow--

When the bar is overhead in the Jerk, Military Press, Push Press or Snatch/Power Snatch, the wrists are commonly bent back. This provides stability overhead by creating a small "bed" for the bar. It also allows you to put the bar a bit more centrally over your front/back base of support.

Wrist and hand position overhead

Elbows

The position of the elbows when taking the bar in your hands at the SET position is unusual in the Olympic-style lifts. It is natural for your elbows to point slightly to the rear when gripping a bar with your palms facing to the rear. However, when performing the Olympic-style lifts, your elbows have to point to the outside, down the line of the bar. This helps assure that the bar stays as close to you as possible during the entire pull and you aren't tempted to reverse curl the bar to your shoulders. It is especially important during the upper portion of the 2nd pull (drive), when the bar is passing your torso, and when the arms start to bend and explosively pull you under the bar to the receiving position. Bad positioning here will lead to the bar moving away from you and will likely lead to not completing the lift.

Make a mental note that your shoulders move slightly forward when turning the elbows to the outside at the Set position. This is an important and correct position to keep in mind.

Correct   *Incorrect*

At the racking of the Clean or Power Clean, the bar should be behind the front deltoids, resting on the collarbones. Your elbows should be pointing directly (or nearly) away from your torso, if possible. As I mentioned earlier, you should have released the "hook" and probably opened your fingers, allowing your elbows to be held higher and making the bar more secure on your shoulders. This higher position of the elbows helps keep the bar from rolling forward off your shoulders and allows you to correctly tighten your torso for the catch and for standing up with the bar. You may be able to achieve this higher elbow position without opening the fingers. This means you have better than average wrist flexibility.

Before attempting the Jerk, Military Press or Push Press, your elbows must be lowered and the bar put in the palms of your hands. This lowering of the elbows makes it easier to put the bar in your palms, which is necessary for better force delivery, and also puts your arms in a more efficient position to deliver force overhead. In addition, it should take the weight of the bar off your arms and put it totally on the torso. If the bar is correctly positioned on the collarbones and behind the front deltoids of the shoulders, optimum delivery of force from your legs and hips during the Jerk and Push Press can be attained.

This lowering of your elbows, along with moving the bar to your palms can be accomplished by a slight, dip and drive of the legs, which should be just enough to momentarily drive the bar off your shoulders. You can make the adjustment while the bar is airborne. You must be careful not to drive the bar too hard and this movement must be vertical in direction. <u>You must stay over the heels when you do this</u>. Practice this movement with empty bar and then progressively heavier weighted bars until you perfect it.

<u>When the bar is overhead in the Jerk or Push Press, your elbows are again pointed down the line of the bar.</u> In the Snatch, this is extremely important to do. If your arms start to twist while a bar is overhead in the Snatch, the bar may simply fall. This is also how injury can occur during this lift, so work on it.

Shoulders

The shoulders are also positioned oddly during the Olympic-style lifts. You are told to keep a straight back when lifting. That might lead you to think that the shoulders are set to the rear, scapulae (shoulder blades) pressed against each other, braced against the weight to be lifted. However, this is not the case. Your shoulders are set <u>slightly forward</u> and <u>stretched slightly downward</u> at the Set position and stay there during the 1st and 2nd pulls (ascending phases) of these lifts. They stay forward in the receiving position for the Clean/Power Clean. They should stay relaxed as well.

Shoulders forward and down at Set   *Shoulders forward at shouldered Clean*

Shoulders up and to the rear in Jerk

The simple explanation for this odd position is that at the Set position for the Clean and the Snatch (and variations), your shoulders move slightly forward of neutral position when the elbows are turned outwards. Keeping your shoulders in this slightly forward and down position allows the muscles there to remain relaxed and ready to react when needed. This positioning also influences how close the bar is during the upper portion of the 2nd pull.

<u>In the racking position for the Clean/Power Clean and Front Squat, your shoulders should be forward of the bar.</u> This helps you keep it on your shoulders and allows your shoulders to stay relaxed before any overhead movements are attempted.

In the overhead portion of the Jerk, Military Press, Push Press and Snatch/Power Snatch, your shoulders are <u>thrust upward</u> and <u>slightly to the rear</u> at the finish. The scapulae (shoulder blades) are pressed together to create a solid base of support for the bar, which is now above your head, and to allow it to be more easily centered over your base of support (front/back).

At the initiation of the 3rd pull (Pull-Under or Slingshot) to the receiving position, certain shoulder muscles contract violently to help accelerate the lifter downwards. If they remained relaxed prior to this, they can deliver a more explosive movement downward.

One other very important thing should be noted about the shoulders. In the Jerk, your shoulders are <u>not thrust upwards</u> to assist the bar leaving the torso but, rather, they are thrust upwards as you punch upward at the bar and descend away from it. Actively lifting your shoulders at the start of the Jerk thrust softens the base of support for the bar at the moment of acceleration, thus limiting it. It also brings the muscle of your arms to bear at too early a stage in the movement and limits your ability to get the shoulders back and up, where they should be.

*****

Quick Gas Station Break

SELF-COACHING RULE: During the Olympic-style lifts, if the bar is below your head, the shoulders are forward of neutral. If the bar is above your head the shoulders are up and back of neutral.

Let's drive down here…oops!

*****

Deadend
How to recognize a BAD strength coach
(A message for athletes and parents)

If your strength coach says any of the following, he is wasting your time.

1. "Never squat below parallel."
2. "Leg extensions are the best leg exercise."
3. "The Smith/Leg Press machine will do you just as good as free weight squatting."
4. "Power cleans really help the upper body and arms."
5. "Olympic lifters aren't strong. They only lift by using momentum."
6. "The bench press is the best exercise for sports."
7. "Catch those Power Cleans like you're doing jumping jacks."
8. "Use sumo deadlifts all the time. They're great for sports."
9. "Bicep curls really improve your power."
10. "I want everything done to failure."
11. "Use the extra wide powerlifting squat. It's great for sports."
12. "Use tight wraps and a suit all the time. They'll save your joints."
13. "Always stay above parallel when you squat."
14. "Power cleans are just a trick."
15. "Step-ups are just as good as squatting."
16. "Machines are just as good as free weights."
17. "Free weights are dangerous."
18. "Weightlifting will make women look like men."

19. "Weightlifters are all those big fat guys that can't move."
20. "Weightlifting will take your flexibility away."
21. "Upper body strength is the most important thing for sports."
22. "I want you to look like a bodybuilder."

*****

What are the 1st, 2nd, and 3rd Pulls?

Now that you have learned the basic Set position and the appropriate hand, elbow and shoulder positions, you should learn the major phases of the Olympic-style lifts: the 1st, 2nd and 3rd pulls. Let's start from the floor and work our way up- and down. Later, I'll discuss the exercises named - *Pulls*.

The 1st Pull: Positioning the Bar

The 1st pull is the portion of the lift in which you drive the bar from the floor and move it towards the Launch Point, which will be moving down to meet the bar with the little double-knee bend trick we spoke of earlier.

You should view the 1st Pull as the set-up for the more explosive 2nd Pull. You move the bar inward and upward at a good but not tremendous pace and accomplish the double-knee bend at as fast a speed as you are capable of while keeping good technique.

Here it is.

1. Get in the Set position (Clean) with you feet balanced toward the front half.
2. Immediately upon pulling the bar from the floor, you drive your knees back, transfer the balance of your feet to the rear and, with a bit of tightening of your latisimus dorsi muscles, squeeze (or sweep) the bar diagonally inward and upward.
3. Continue to drive upward with knee extension being the major mover.
4. Your torso should bow over the bar slightly and your arms will be pointing diagonally back and down just before the double-knee bend.
5. Initiate the double-knee bend by allowing your knees to go forward, while staying over the heels.
6. At the same time, extend your hips slightly to keep the bar rising during the downward movement of your hips, due to the re-bending of your knees.

1st Pull

At this point, the 1st Pull is, for all intent, over. You have gotten the bar to the Launch Point and you are set up for the greatest explosive effort in all of sports. And, your hip extension is going to catapult the bar upward at a tremendous rate of speed.

The 2nd Pull: The Catapult

I view the 2nd Pull as an explosive catapulting of the bar upward toward your shoulders, in the Clean/Power Clean or overhead, in the Snatch/Power Snatch. This is simply my term to describe what happens as the hips extend at full acceleration and act on the bar. To me, this action is what launches the bar upward, just as a catapult launches its projectile downfield. The major difference is twofold. First, this catapult launches a very heavy load a few inches upward and second, you catch the projectile you just catapulted upward. When you are performing the 2nd Pull mimicking the catapult, there is no need for you to consciously add to the force of the hip extension to perform the Olympic lifts correctly.

Here it is.

1. With the bar at the Launch Point and your bodyweight still balanced over your heels, you begin to extend your hips explosively <u>upward</u>.
2. As you proceed, you attempt to accelerate.
3. As you drive the bar upward, you will naturally move slightly forward onto the front of your feet.
4. As the force of your hip extension causes your (most people) heels to leave the floor, you push outward through the balls of your feet to the stance in which you will receive the bar.

2nd Pull

It is important to realize that this all takes place in a matter of less than a second. The bar will be driven upward (and slightly outward) into the air and, with the initiation of the 3rd Pull, will be brought to your shoulders or placed overhead. There you have the most powerful movement in all of sports.

*****

COACHES: There is a fair amount of dissention about the end of the 2nd Pull. Some think more time is spent on the balls of the feet at the end of the 2nd Pull and you should attempt to deliver more force to the bar in this position by pushing upward through the feet and shrugging the bar up as well. I feel that this is a waste of time and that when you reach the balls of your feet, you should be pushing them outward to the receiving position and starting the transition to the downward movement of your body. It is this immediate, downward acceleration while holding a heavy implement that sets this task apart from all other sports movements and demands different use of the body's levers and musculature.

Some very good lifters never move their heels off the floor. Some only move their feet off the floor as the force of the hip extension lifts them up, but never plantar flex. More often, movement into plantar flexion is only necessary for lifters to move their feet to a receiving position. Hip extension is dominant in Olympic-style lifting as the source of force on the bar and many do not need to plantar flex at all to finish the movement efficiently.

Some athletes may actually start to push off backward at the transition from the 2nd to the 3rd pull. This can be purposeful and result in very good lifts. Moving the feet to the rear can also mean there is a flaw in the pull. If the position of the torso is leaned overly forward at the catch, the jump back is not for a good reason. If the landing in the 3rd pull is solid, and the torso is more upright, the backward jump is fine.

The 3rd Pull: The Pull-Under
(The Slingshot)

Whether you are performing the classic Olympic lifts or their variations, correct technique when pulling under the bar is essential. Your final receiving position may be different (high catch, low catch, split, etc.) but the basic technique of reaching those positions is the same.

A basic concept to understand is that as the bar, which has been catapulted from the hips, is approaching the apex of its flight, it is slowing down. As it slows, it "weighs more," and you can use this slowing bar to pull yourself to a lower position quickly, almost as if it was attached to the floor. You can, in fact, accelerate yourself downward faster than the speed of gravity. The bar, no matter how heavily it is loaded can only descend at the speed of gravity. You are not limited by such constraints. With the correct timing and technique, you can get beneath the bar and be set to catch it when it gets there. The timing of the transition from driving the bar upward to pulling yourself downward is crucial in performing the Olympic-style lifts. It is misunderstood and neglected by many and is more of a cause of not lifting heavier weights as any other aspect of the total technique.

You should start to pull under the bar as soon as full hip extension is achieved. To wait any longer slows the motion in the transition and that is not acceptable.

Here's the quick and dirty explanation of the 3rd pull.

1. Move the feet to the floor with the heels getting to the ground quickly.
2. Contract your trapezius, and arms by flexion of the elbows, starting you downward.
3. While the accelerative descent continues, try to keep your torso as upright as possible.
4. As you descend, rotate your elbows forward and start the action of receiving the bar.
5. When you have reached your squat or Power position, keep pressure on the bar, up through the torso, when shouldered and through the arms and retracted scapulae, when overhead.

Pull-under and result

Your feet should always go to the same width (approx. hip width at the heels) to catch the bar. If the bar hasn't been driven as high, due to greater weight, pull the hips lower instead of spreading the feet wider. You should always be trying to get your heels down quickly.

As you reach the final receiving position for the Clean/Power Clean, your arms wrap around the bar, ending with your elbows pointing forward and, in most cases, slightly to the outside. In the Snatch/Power Snatch, your arms are straight and above the back of your head, your shoulders are elevated, and your shoulder blades are retracted.

Let's move on to the drills that will teach you proper, modern Olympic weightlifting technique. Remember, no matter what your sport, these lifts will help you more than anything else you can do in the weight room. Learn to use the techniques that the best weightlifters in the world use and you will gain an advantage over all your competitors.

CHAPTER III: The Ten-Step Method

This is the method I use with new lifters. You may find that you have lifters that are far enough along to skip some of the earlier steps. I strongly suggest that no one, whether you have been lifting for two days or two years skip past Step Five. To me, this is vital and it will be foreign to most lifters in this country.

Step 1: Full depth Air Squats
(Hip joint below knee joint)

Stand in front of the mirror (side to it) again, with your feet flat and pointed slightly outwards. Your <u>heels</u> should be approximately hip width apart. This foot position simply gives your hips room to descend between your feet with the torso more or less upright. Some people can squat below parallel perfectly fine with their feet closer, but for our purposes right now, try it a bit wider.

Before we start, let's go over a couple of things that are true in all types of squatting.

1. Before each squat repetition, you should be balanced over your heels and descend through them, drifting downwards at first by <u>allowing</u> your knees to go forward and then, near the bottom slowing the descent by tightening your glutes.
2. At the start of the descent, feel like you're sticking your "tailbone" backwards while trying to keep your chest pointing forward.
3. Of course, with any squat, come up faster than you went down and don't "bounce" out of the bottom position.
4. Your bodyweight will naturally shift slightly towards the front of your feet when ascending from the bottom position toward standing as your hips press forward and upwards and the quads come more into play (above parallel). Make sure when this happens that it is limited to just past mid-foot and you raise the torso in a manner to move the balance back toward the heels as you finish the movement.
5. For the purpose of this drill, come to a straight-legged position at the top of each repetition and reset onto your heels before starting the next descent.

In future Back and Front Squat workouts, rise to straight legs but do not regularly lock your knees. Sometimes locking the knees is needed for you to take a rest or help to re-balance the bar.

One more thing before we start the drill. Make sure you are wearing shoes that have a heel height higher than the sole under the front of the shoe. Most people need this to squat correctly. Proper weightlifting shoes are built in this manner. If you don't have such a shoe, use a ¼" to ½" lift under the heel portion of the your shoes to help with your balance (a strip of ½" rubber or wood will do nicely).

At first running shoes will do but proper shoes will become necessary to provide more stability during all weightlifting movements. Cheap, low-cut work boots will do fine as your first weightlifting shoe.

Now, athletes, do this:

1. Extend your arms forward, palms down, parallel to the floor.
2. Place your bodyweight over your heels.
3. Stay over your heels, tighten your abs, take a breath in and descend slowly by allowing your hips to flex, your knees to go forward in the line that your feet are pointing until your hips are lower than your knees while trying to keep your arms forward and parallel to the floor. Your back will tilt forward slightly as you descend which is fine as long as it is straight; and your arms will likely rise a bit, which is also fine for now.
4. Immediately return to the standing position, starting the drive upwards through your heels, then through the mid-foot and, than, back to heels until you are almost straight legged once again. You may breath out when above parallel during the assent.
5. If all is balanced, do another repetition. If not, you should remain at the straight leg position and place your bodyweight over the heels once again and then start to descend.
6. **Do three sets of ten-twelve repetitions, pausing at the low point of two or three repetitions.**
7. Then, do two more sets of ten, holding your hands behind your head, fingers interlocked, pausing at the low point of two or three repetitions.

Start/finish and low point of Air Squat

I <u>do not</u> suggest using a short box behind you to sit down to as a cue to let you know when you have reached the bottom of the squat. I consider this a dangerous thing to do because of the likelihood of sitting down hard on the box and injuring your back. If you need a prop to provide you with a tactile cue for depth, try a med ball and just barely touch it when sitting in the low squat position.

Of course, my coach used to tell me to imagine "a white hot knitting needle right under your a--". But those "Old School" visualizations are somewhat frowned upon in this era of Political Correctness. I'll tell you one thing though: I always, always started up from the bottom of squats quickly. I never fell to the bottom position and tried to bounce out. Nor did I fail to get up with many. It gave new meaning to the phrase "touch and go" for me.

Don't bounce or rebound out of the bottom of the full squat and make sure your back is remaining straight throughout. Bouncing is a sign that you don't know how to tighten your glutes to slow a descent in the squat. You are still trying to use some momentum from a bounce at the bottom to get up high enough for your quads to take over and to be on the front of the foot to recover from the bottom position. This will likely cause knee injury and could cause back injury. And, it is simply bad form. Make sure you use light weights until you understand the concept of how to use your glutes to slow the descent near the bottom and start the ascent from a below parallel position. You must understand that the ascent starts through the rear of the feet and with the contraction of the glutes.

Pull over for a minute.

*****

Quick Gas Station Break

COACHES: Coaching cues throughout this drill (and most others) should be shot-gunned at athletes. You never know which one will work but if you throw enough out there, you're bound to hit 'em with something. And, I don't want to hear about lifters who say they've got to have quiet to concentrate. If your lifters can't put up with your voice, how will they ever put up with the chaos of competition? This ain't golf.

1. "Sit down."
2. "Stick your butt out back."
3. "Keep your chest forward."
4. "Don't look down."
5. "Down slow! Up fast."
6. "Sit through your heels."
7. "Keep your abs tight."
8. "Breathe out near the top."
9. "Drive your knees back."
10. "Didn't I tell you not to look down?!"

These all might be used and other of the more infamous "expletives deleted" type exhortations may be used as well. The important thing is to get the athlete to do it right and make it memorable. Their muscles will "remember". You make sure their brains do, as well. As you and your athletes get more "in tune" with each other, less will have to be said.

Back to the Highway.

Step 2: The Muscle Snatch

I think it's best to learn the Power Snatch and Snatch before the Power Clean or Clean. My reasoning is that with the Snatch grip, the Launch Point for the bar is put at the hip level and you learn how to use the hip extension better with the bar in contact with the hips. Hip extension is the star of the show, folks. The hips are the Center of Power in the human body.

I don't use a lot of the Muscle Snatch exercise in my workout programs because it slows down at the top of the 2nd pull and it reinforces using the arms to pull the bar upwards, neither of which happen in the actual Olympic-style lifts. It can be used to strengthen the shoulders but I prefer to do that with other lifts. I don't like you practicing things that you shouldn't be doing and feeling in the actual Olympic-style lifts. Some lifters do like to use it as a warm-up for the shoulders.

That said, it is a lift that can be used initially to show what the line of a Snatch/Power Snatch should be when it travels by the torso and is put into the final catch position. And that's why it's here, near the beginning of my progression towards doing the Power Snatch and Snatch.

Very simply, Athletes:

1. Hold the bar (dowel) at your hips, using the snatch grip. Always use a light dowel or bar.
2. Stand with slightly flexed hips and knees, allowing the bar to slide down your thighs a bit and, with little forceful hip extension help, lift the bar to a position over the back of your head with arms fully extended and shoulders reaching up and slightly back. While pulling the bar up, try to keep shoulders forward slightly and keep the dowel close to your torso throughout. You will pull the dowel upwards using your arms and bending elbows towards the ceiling until you finally pull it upwards into a position above the back of your head.
3. Do not re-bend your knees when putting the bar in its final position above the head.
4. Loosen your elbows and, maintaining the same grip, curl your wrists forward and allow the bar to travel back down the path it traveled upward. Bend you knees and hips a bit to absorb the shock of the bar coming to rest on your thighs.
5. Do several sets of six to eight repetitions of this to teach yourself the approximate line of the bar at this point of the pull.

CHAPTER III: The Ten-Step Method

The Muscle Snatch

Step 3: The Overhead Squat
(Now, the fun really starts)

This squat is to be done to full depth and is important, not only to practicing the final receiving position of the Squat Snatch but as a great exercise for improving your strength, flexibility, balance and spatial awareness. It is especially important for Olympic weightlifters and throwers (discus, hammer, etc.) to learn this exercise. But all athletes can benefit from it. And, it is essential in learning proper form for the Snatch.

1. Perform an Air Squat as in step #1, except with your hands clasped behind your head.
2. Then, do an Air Squat with your arms above your head (angled slightly outward).
3. Now, holding a dowel (or light tech bar) with the Snatch grip, put it over your head fully extending the elbows. Keep the bar at full arms length throughout the movement and descend to a point <u>below parallel</u> (hips below knees) staying

flat-footed. (You might use a large med ball as a prop to touch with your glutes at the "bottom" of the squat, when first learning how low to go.)
4. If you can do this and maintain the bar position above the back of your head, do several sets of 5-10 repetitions and pause some of them at the bottom of the squat, as well, so you will remember the feeling of the positions.

Start/finish and low point of Overhead Squat

Remember, all squats start the descent through your heels and start the ascent through the heels. The balance on your feet travels forward to the balls of the feet in the middle portion of the lift and then should be shifted back again near the top of the lift.

If you cannot do this correctly, do Steps 1-3 and then:

1. Sit on a small, cushioned bench or chair that places your hips lower than your knees. Keeping your back straight and slightly tilted, place a light bar above your head in the snatch position.
2. Position your feet as you would for an Air Squat and, keeping the bar in position, stand up.
3. Descend carefully to the chair but <u>barely touch it</u> and return to the standing position.

You may have to use a higher chair and some of you may only be able to do one repetition at a time or even only the ascent portion of the movement starting from the chair or bench. Be patient and get it right. You will. As soon as you can do more than one repetition, start from the standing position and descend carefully to the chair. As soon as possible, replace the chair with the med ball prop I mentioned above. Then, of course, remove the med ball and do the exercise, free of props.

You can now can sit to the bottom position of the snatch correctly and recover to a standing position. This is no small accomplishment.

For those of you not interested in learning the Full Squat Snatch, this lift is still very valuable for balance and flexibility reasons. Football players, throwers, wrestlers and goalies for all sports should get very good at Overhead Squats. And, again, it is essential in this progression.

Step 4: The Drop Snatch
(Snatch Balance)

I will always call this the Drop Snatch because, many, many, many years ago when I learned it, that's what it was called. So, in this book, that's what it will be called. Most other books will refer to it as the Snatch Balance.

Basically, it is a drill to teach you to go to the full squat quickly with the bar in the Snatch grip above your head. It is often taught, along with some other variations, as a step in learning the full Snatch. I would rather introduce it here as sort of the fast-first cousin to the Overhead Squat since neither of them has upward momentum of the bar involved*, as there will be in the actual snatch lifts. At this point, the lift should be done with a wooden or plastic dowel or a very light training bar.

The lift starts with the you standing straight and holding the bar on the back of your shoulders with your hands in the Snatch grip position and your feet at the distance apart they would be at the Set position for this lift. Your balance on your feet should be slightly to the front.

Giving no upward momentum to the bar, the you should simultaneously drop away from it, spread your feet to the squat position used in the Overheads and punch your arms upwards until full elbow extension is attained (and maintained throughout) and the bar is secured over the back of your head. The result should be that you catch the bar above your head with arms straight and locked at the elbows while landing flat-footed (get your heels down) and attaining a full or partial squat.

Once that is done, stand up to your original position with the bar still at arm's length and then replacing the bar on the back of your shoulders and prepare to do the next repetition.

* There is a variation of this lift in which a bit of a dip and drive is used at the start, giving the bar a bit of upward momentum before the lifter descends. This is usually used by Olympic weightlifters when doing this exercise with very heavy weights. I do not suggest you use this method when performing this lift unless you are doing very heavy weight and I don't suggest using heavy weights for this exercise unless you are an Olympic weightlifter or a thrower. If you use this variation, the dip and drive is initiated <u>through the heels</u>.)

This is it, step by step.

1. Take bar (dowel, at first) from rack, placing it on your back as you would a back squat.
2. Step out of the racks and place your hands at the correct Snatch grip position.
3. Set your feet as you would in the Set position, as described earlier (bodyweight over <u>the front of the feet</u>).
4. Simultaneously, drop away from the bar, punch your arms upward and drive through the sides of your feet to the wider squat position you used for the Overheads, landing on <u>flat feet</u>. Make sure your heels get down and you descend through them.
5. After stabilizing in a full or partial squat position, stand up.
6. To lower the bar to your back, pump your legs slightly and slide your hands inwards to nearly the Clean grip. Don't let the bar leave your hands.
7. Loosen your elbows and bring the bar down to the back of your shoulders. (Bending your knees slightly will absorb the impact of the bar on your shoulders).
8. Stand up and reset your feet to the Set stance and your hands in the snatch grip positions and repeat.

Start   *Descent*   *Catch*   *Finish*

Do this for several sets of 4-6 repetitions for the purpose of this drill.

As a training lift, most athletes should use the same repetitions, but will use heavier weight than we will use here. Heavy doubles or singles are probably only helpful for Olympic Weightlifters.

It is important, to get your heels back to the floor when widening to the squat position. You want to always land <u>flat-footed</u> and you want the glutes to be in control at the bottom of a squat. Also, this is a great time to practice that up and back motion of the shoulders that will happen in the Snatch. Squeeze those shoulder blades (scapulae) together and reach up with the shoulders as the bar nears its final position overhead.

The positions you will reach at the bottom of this lift should be duplicated in your full squat Snatch later. There is no reason to have to lean the torso forward much more than you are doing in the Drop Snatch than during a full Squat Snatch. If you do, you're probably doing something wrong during the performance of the actual lift.

The Drop Snatch will teach you that you <u>CAN ALWAYS BEAT THE BAR TO THE FINISH</u> (receiving position) during an actual Snatch. If you keep your wits about you, accelerate yourself downwards by pulling yourself under the bar and then punch your arms upwards, you'll always be ready to catch a bar when it finally descends because you'll already be there in a strong receiving position, waiting for it. Physics is on your side. You're moving faster than gravity is bringing the bar downward. And, one more bit of information. It won't matter what the weight is on the bar because we all know that the speed of gravity is constant.

Note: Those using the Split Style can also do this lift. All things remain the same except, of course, you go to the split instead of the squat. It is shown on the DVD.

Step 5: Let's Rock and Roll*and Learn the Olympic Lifts
(2nd Pull (Drive) Preparatory Drill)

You know enough now to try learning the actual Olympic lifts. Let's get to it with the drill that is critical to learning proper technique and the first drill we've done that closely mimics the movements and the rhythm of the acceleration in the 2nd pull, starts at the Launch Point and leads naturally into the transition to the receiving position.

The Rock&Roll also tends to naturally lead people to being able to perform a natural "double-knee bend" because your knees straighten during the first part of this exercise and then bend again as you return the balls of your feet to the floor. The mysterious "double-knee bend" is really the same movement only it doesn't involve lifting the balls of your feet off the floor when doing it. This is really an exercise that you want to do while watching the DVD. Watching people do this will help you more than any words I can write.

IMPORTANT: The tendency, at first, in this exercise is to swing or loop the bar away from the torso. As in all the Olympic-style lifts, this is wrong. The bar has to be kept as close to the torso as possible as it passes. This will minimize the movement of the bar away from you in the second pull. "Up through your shirt" and "Keep your elbows out." are the classic cues. You, as the lifter, must always be thinking that you will try to drive your hips and the bar upward.

Remember, in the snatch or the clean grip, the elbows are to be pointing outward, towards the ends of the bar. When the arms do "pull" you under the bar, the elbows are to go towards the ceiling as much as possible and you should be on your way to the receiving position.

I named this drill the Rock & Roll so you could remember it, but my friend Coach Shin Ho Kang, former Korean Head International Coach taught it to me. It had no name he could tell me, but it is taught to novice lifters in Korea. It teaches speed, rhythm, balance and the use of hip extension as the primary mover of the bar by using a quick, exaggerated movement that simulates the general movement of the legs, back and hips just before and through the accelerative portion of the lift, and brings you through the receiving phase as well. It sets the rhythmic and movement stage for becoming competent at both the power and full squat versions of the classic Olympic lifts. I think it's great fun.

Note: A crucial and somewhat difficult skill you need to perform this lift is the ability to lift the front of your feet in the air, thrust your butt toward the rear and lean forward at the same time, balanced only on your heels. If this baffles you, try grabbing a pole or something attached to the floor and practicing the movement before trying the Rock & Roll. Or, have a buddy face you and hold your hands and anchor you while you get into this position.

CHAPTER III: The Ten-Step Method

Learn to be on your heels

The term **Launch Point** describes the placement of the bar during this drill. You remember it is the point on your body that you want the bar to be in contact with when you initiate the explosive second pull in the Snatch or the Clean. One of the great things about the Rock&Roll drill is that it teaches the lifter where that point is, and the direction in which the lifter wants to deliver force in order to make the bar go to the correct position above the head.

I want to make it clear that this is a DRILL to help you with the lift and that in the actual lift, the front of the feet do not lift up off the floor during the middle of the pull. Remember, this is a drill lift that teaches by using exaggeration of movement and position.

Part A

1. Start by standing straight with a wooden dowel (or PVC "rattle stick") using the Snatch grip.
2. Tilt over slightly and bend your knees, keeping the bar against your hips (Launch Point for the Snatch), your torso straight and your weight on your heels but still flat-footed with your feet slightly closer than hip width (or in your established set position stance, if you're a veteran lifter)
3. Holding the bar against your hips and with your back straight, stick your tailbone out to the rear until your forefeet come off the floor. During this phase,

your torso should tilt over (back remains straight) and your legs will straighten somewhat. Do NOT go to locked knees here.
4. Then, bring your hips forward, causing the forefeet to return to the floor, and start to raise your torso quickly.
5. At the instant your forefeet touch the floor and with your balance still over the rear of your feet, explosively drive the hips upward and inward, catapulting the bar upward, bring the torso to vertical and drive the bar overhead, then use your traps and arms (elbow bend upwards) to pull yourself to the high receiving position with slightly bent knees.
6. "Catch" the bar in a position vertically above the back of your head, with bent knees and flat feet (balance mid-foot), now shuffled* out slightly wider than they started and chest pointing forward. (By the way, on your way through this movement, you have now performed a Power Snatch from a very high hanging position.)
7. Now, bring the bar down, return to the starting position and do it again and again and again. Do three to four sets of ten.

Start through finish of Rock and Roll

* In all Olympic lifts and these drills as well, almost all people will "jump out" to the receiving position. This is NOT a jump or a push through the floor to drive the bar upward. That doesn't happen here and shouldn't happen in the actual lifts. This happens after the major part of the explosive hip extension has occurred and is part of the transition to slingshotting yourself under the bar to the receiving position. Ideally, this foot movement looks more like a shuffle and your feet barely leave the floor. It is important to get your feet (flat) back in contact with the floor as quickly as possible at this time.

The keys to this exercise and most lifting are:
    a.   Slow to fast
    b.   Keep the bar close

CHAPTER III: The Ten-Step Method

        c.   Keep your eyes forward
        d.   Start hip explosion from the heels (or close)
        e.   Reach up when the bar is overhead
        f.   Don't jump into the air
        g.   THINK FROM YOUR HIPS
        h.   PUSH THROUGH YOUR HEELS AS MUCH AS POSSIBLE

When doing this exercise, the weight used in the beginning is very light. It is <u>THE</u> critical technical assistance exercise that will open up the road to all Olympic lifting to you. Don't try to see how much you can lift this way. Later, some weight can be added but I don't believe you should ever do this exercise with even moderately heavy weight. The intent of this exercise is to learn how the hips drive the bar, where to drive it from, and the rhythm and positions entering and executing the explosive second pull. This drill can be done every training day with beginners and probably should be done at least once every week even with very experienced athletes.

When you master this lift, the rest will flow downhill like water. Understanding that explosive hip extension is what really accelerates the bar, (not knee or ankle extension) and how to "feel" it is the key to lifting. Explosive hip extension is the key to all power movements in sports, whether it is throwing a discus or hitting a golf ball or making a great tackle. The only difference between the body actions in delivering power in most sports and delivering power in the Olympic-style lifts is that in most sports the direction of the athlete (or implement) is forward as well as upward to complete their movements, so there is much more forefoot involvement and more conscious and forceful knee and ankle extension.

When performing the Olympic-style lifts, the task is not just to deliver force to the bar but for the athlete to reverse his direction and end up beneath it and catch it. This unique task causes the lifter to minimize the last phase of triple extension (plantar flexion), and to change the object and direction of force delivery to himself and his downward movement around the bar during this transition.

In fact, plantar flexion has proven to be unnecessary, as long as the athlete can change direction efficiently without it. Athletes who do this are fully in control of their hip extension and produce tremendous power with this movement. Their muscular development and balance has been thoroughly formed to move rhythmically to the finish of the lift with no extraneous movements.

All athletes who train using the Olympic-style lifts should understand that if proper form is maintained and if your conscious effort is on complete and aggressive hip extension, the bar will be driven high enough for you to catch in a solid position. The Olympic-style lifts will give you the ability, like nothing else, to move great weight, very fast, to where you want it to go.

And, it should be noted that, in any sport, if hip extension is not strong and well controlled, athletic performance will suffer greatly. Athletes without it will be more likely to have recurring injuries, especially to the knees and ankle joints and to the back, all of which are put under undo stress if the hips aren't strong and able to lead the way through athletic movements.

COACHES: Pushing or staying "through the heels" refers to the idea of driving up through the rear of the foot through the first pull and staying there through the "scoop" portion of the lift. Also, as a cue, I like to tell lifters to feel as though they are staying "through the heels" for the entire ascending portion of the lifts. This is blatantly not true, but it can help lifters from straying too far forward on their base of support while lifting, which is a bad mistake during these lifts.

*****

Part B

Mid-Rock and Roll Power Snatch

I want you to do the first portion of the Rock & Roll and STOP when you get your forefeet back down on the floor. Check your position and balance. You should have the bar still in contact with your hips (Snatch Launch Point). Your shoulders should be in front of the bar and your torso should be tilted slightly forward. Your back should be straight and your shoulders should be forward of neutral, with your elbows pointing outwards. Your balance should still be over the rear half of your feet with your heels in contact with the floor (platform). The front of your feet should be touching the floor with no downward force being delivered.

Now, from this position:
1. Drive your hips up and forward and bring your torso to vertical quickly.
2. Pull yourself under the elevating bar to the high (Power) receiving position.
3. Practice this for several sets of three to five repetitions.

Doing these repetitions from this point of the Rock & Roll drill will result in a Power Snatch from a high hang (Launch Point) position. If you can, proceed to the full squat or split position here and do that for three to five sets of two repetitions.

Step 6: Ready, Set and Sweep the Bar
(1st Pull (Drive) Preparatory Drill)

This is the most important drill for learning how to set yourself and start the bar off the floor. Basically, it is a light, partial Olympic-style Deadlift* initiated from the clean or snatch set positions. In this drill, the torso <u>never reaches vertical</u>. In fact, it bows slightly as the bar moves toward the Launch Point.

*An Olympic-style Deadlift, as I define it, is one that is initiated from the same Set position as the Clean or Snatch pull and is swept inwards as an actual pull in an Olympic lift is. Also, your back will tilt over more as the deadlift moves upwards, just as the back does in an Olympic-style pull. The back is straightened to vertical in a complete Olympic-style Deadlift.

Ready

Approach the bar and, standing over it, look down. You should see (imagine you have X-ray vision) your big toe on the far side of the bar. You are now close enough to the bar to lift it correctly. When you set yourself, your shins may or may not touch the bar. This depends on flexibility at the ankle, length of your shinbone and other variables. <u>Make sure, as you set yourself down on the bar that it stays over the base of your toes.</u>

Set

Get into the Set position discussed earlier.

Sweep it in
(The BIG secret)

CHAPTER III: The Ten-Step Method 103

Start, mid-point and finish of Sweep Drill

Initiate the partial Olympic Deadlift by moving the balance on your feet from the front to the rear as you drive your knees to the rear and *sweeping* the bar inward by tightening your lats. I covered this earlier, but I think everyone needs as many cues about this technique as a coach can get into a session. It takes a bit of getting used to but it is quite easy once you do it a few times. When you sweep the bar in, be sure your shoulders remain forward of a neutral position and the lats initiate the sweeping motion by a slight contraction or squeezing. This will cause the bar to move diagonally towards you.

If you are having trouble understanding how to do this "sweep using your lats" thing, try standing with your arms hanging straight by your sides, palms to the rear, elbows out and shoulders slightly forward. Have a partner hold your shoulder in a slightly forward of neutral position and put his other hand in the palm of your hand and offer a slight forward pressure. Push back against the pressure, keeping your arm straight.

Let's try the Snatch version first.

1. Get to the Set position (balance on the front of your feet) and put your hands at your snatch width grip.
2. Tighten abs and take a small breath and start driving the bar from the floor, making sure your knees are traveling towards the rear forcefully and imagine yourself pushing your shins down through your heels.
3. Squeeze your lats and sweep the bar inwards toward you. (2 and 3 together should put the bar on a diagonal drive line coming towards the lifter)
4. As you drive the bar from the floor, try to maintain the torso angle of the set position until it passes knee height.
5. As the bar approaches the Launch Point at the hips, the torso angle will tilt forward, slightly towards the horizontal.
6. As the bar touches the front of your hips (it will touch your upper thighs in the Clean version), reverse the direction of the bar and return it to the floor, backtracking down the same pathway and moving through the same torso angles you moved through on the ascent.
7. Barely touch the bar (plates) to the floor and do it again and again and again.
8. Do not try for speed but a controllable rhythm during this exercise.
9. You should be thinking "stay through your heels" (really rear of feet) throughout the pulling and descending portions of this drill, only allowing your bodyweight to be over the forefeet only after you arrive at the Set position to start over.
10. Your shoulders maintain their relaxed, slightly forward, position.
11. Your head should be forward and relaxed throughout (angled with torso acceptable).
12. No "scoop" or "double knee bend" is performed in this drill.

I think this first pull drill should be done using the Snatch grip. If you find it easier to use the Clean grip and Set position instead, that is fine. You will be doing it from both Set positions soon.

COACHES: Here's that exercise that might help you get the idea of "sweeping" across to your athletes. It's called the Prone Sweep and is done as follows.

Have the athlete lie in the prone position on a freestanding bench, hanging his head off the end and allowing his shoulders to droop around the sides. Using dumbbells and keeping his arms straight and palms toward the feet, have him sweep the dumbbells back and up until his arms are just below parallel to the floor. Have your athlete do this for three to four sets of eight to twelve repetitions. It will reinforce that sweeping motion

The athlete's shoulders should remain "drooped" because they're forward and relaxed in the pull. The head should also be relaxed throughout this exercise. This exercise can be done with an Olympic bar beneath the bench as well but the bar will come up and hit the bottom of the bench. I have used the cue of hitting the bottom of the bench to teach lifters the idea of the sweep.

Step 7: Partial Deadlift/Stop and Shift/Power Snatch

I like you to do this drill using the snatch grip first because that will put the bar right on your hips (pubic bone, really-Launch Point for the snatch). I believe that constantly putting the emphasis on hip extension as the primary mover in these lifts is critical. We are now simply going to combine the two moves we've just learned into one. First, you will do it with a pause in the middle and then without one. Below are the steps for combining these drills.

(Use a dowel or a very light tech bar. And, do some Rock & Rolls right beforehand, stopping for a second in the middle of that drill when your feet are flat on the floor having returned to the platform and, then, finish the movement.)

Here we go:

1. Take your correct Snatch **SET** position at the floor.
2. Do the Partial Deadlift/Sweep and <u>STOP</u> at the Launch Point (hips), keeping feet flat.
3. From that position, SHIFT to the position you are in when you put the front of your feet down again in the R&R, drive the bar to the correct position overhead for the Power Snatch.
4. Reset your feet and do it again. This time try not to stop for the shift at your hips.
5. Repeat this couplet (one stopping and one not) several times.
6. Do this drill in sets of five to ten couplets.

Partial Dead to Power Snatch catch

By combining the Partial Olympic-style Deadlift and Sweep through the first pull and the explosive Catapulting portion of the Rock and Roll drill during the second pull, you are now doing a basic Power Snatch. Remember that in all actual lifts, the <u>feet remain flat on the</u>

floor during the transition from the 1st and 2nd pulls and that lifting the front of the feet is only a part of the Rock & Roll drill done earlier. It is also very important to realize that the PAUSE at the hips before the explosive second pull is also NOT present in actual lifts. You must work to fade that pause in this drill as quickly as possible.

As in all actual lifts, the balancing point on your feet will shift in these drills. At the SET position, the balance is over the front of the feet, except for those who start with their shoulders behind the bar. As you start the bar from the floor and push knees back to extend, the balance goes to the heels. And, although the second drive explosion will be initiated from the heels (rear of feet), balance will again go slightly to the front as hip extension occurs and the bar is catapulted upward and slightly outward.

Also, thinking of cues like "move slow to fast", "every move is faster than the last one until it's done" and "stay ahead of the bar" might be ones that work for you when learning this sequence and, in fact, all three might work for you all the time.

Step 8: Now, the Full Snatch (Squat-style) from the Launch Point, Hang and from the Floor

The most difficult aspect of doing the full squat version of the Snatch is that a fair amount of natural shoulder, hip, knee and ankle flexibility are necessary to reach a solid, final receiving position. If, however, you diligently do the drills we have gone over earlier, you should increase your flexibility and coordination in the positions and movements needed. Some of you may have already been able to accomplish this step of the progression earlier. If so, do this for practice anyway. For the rest, let's try to get to this squat (or low split) position right from the Launch Point. The mechanics of learning how to the squat version of the lifts, if you've done the Rock & Roll many times and are doing it correctly, are not that hard.

First, warm up for this by doing two to three sets of light Overhead Squats w/Snatch grip. Then, move on to do two to three sets of Drop Snatches (Snatch Balance) with light bar. And, finally move on to doing some Rock & Rolls.

Do this drill with a dowel or a Rattle Stick or a very light Tech bar, only.

Full Snatch from the Launch Point:

1. Do two to three Snatch grip R&R's and at the receiving position of the last one, pause, then go down through your flat feet (through heels) at the receiving position to full depth Overhead Squat position you learned earlier.
2. Do several sets of this, only pausing momentarily at the top, before going into the Overhead Squat. You must emphasize sitting down through your heels when descending into the Overhead Squat.
3. If you do this and can go down to at least a parallel squat, start attempting to eliminate the slight pause and go right into the squat after completing the Rock & Roll movement.
4. Now, stop the R&R when your feet return to the flat position after being balanced on your heels. Count to 3. Complete the rest of the R&R movement and continue to the full Snatch position.

Do several sets of three to five repetitions, if this movement is starting to feel comfortable. If you do not feel like this is working well, go back to Step # 3 and start through again. Take a break first.

If you have had real trouble from the start getting any kind of a parallel or below squat, even in the Overhead Squatting section, it might be time to consider using the Split catching position for the full movements.

Full Squat Snatch from the Hang

Continue to use light bar or dowel for this exercise right now.

CHAPTER III: The Ten-Step Method

This may be the hardest lift in this section. Not because you can't squat or don't know how to catapult a weight by now, but because of the starting position and the movements immediately at the start of this lift.

1. Lower the bar, still gripping it with your Snatch grip, to your knees.
2. Set your shoulders in exactly the position they would be in if you were starting the bar from the floor. (directly over the bar)
3. Start the movement by sweeping the bar inward and moving your knees back, just as you would from the floor and allow your back to tilt over, keeping the bar swept in.
4. Drive towards the Launch Point and allow your knees to come forward as you raise your back. (scoop)
5. Catapult the bar from the Launch Point to the Power Snatch position overhead.
6. Pause for a moment, if you have to, and then go into a full squat Snatch position.
7. Do the lift from the knees again and try to eliminate the Pause at the top.

Snatch from the Hang

The hard part is making yourself go through the movements that you would from the floor, when the bar is in a hanging position. Your brain will tell you to simply fire upward from the point at which the bar is hanging. This is wrong, as I discussed earlier in the book. <u>You must put the legs, hips and back through the same sequence of movements they will go through when lifting a bar from the floor, when doing a hang from anywhere below the Launch Point.</u>

Watch the DVD for a visual on this lift. It will help you immensely.

Full Squat Snatch From the Floor

This can be even more difficult than the first drill but, if you have completed the Rock & Roll drill (2nd pull), the Partial Deadlift/Sweep drill (1st pull), and the combination of the two, it should not be that hard to go on to a smooth Full Squat Snatch from the floor.

Now, here we go:

1. Do the Partial Dead./Sweep from the Set position, Shift and go through the Rock & Roll (flat-footed version) without stopping and to the receiving position of your basic Power Snatch.
2. Do this for several sets of 3-5.
3. Do an Overhead Squat after "catching" the Power Snatch, with only a minimal pause.
4. Try again to go to the squat without any pause at the top.

CHAPTER III: The Ten-Step Method

Start, Launch and Catch of Squat Snatch

Just as always, you should be thinking of getting down to flat feet in the squat as quickly as possible after the extension. You should be able to accomplish this but, if you can't, take your time, do a few Overhead Squats and try again to work through this sequence. If it is really difficult for you to come close to getting reasonable positions, you may have to try the Split positions I spoke of above. They're on the DVD. Or, you may just have to take a break for lunch or come back and try tomorrow. These are difficult movements, and although I think this is a superior way to learn them, it will not be simple.

Step 9: Power Clean Rock & Roll

Part A

Doing the Rock and Roll with the Clean grip begins with the bar below most people's hips. This is the Launch Point for the Power Clean and Clean and is lower due to the closer handgrip. Additionally, the bar is going to end up on your shoulders rather than overhead as with the Snatch. The Clean Rock & Roll will be performed as we did before, and the second pull will begin from where it contacts your upper thighs. Pay particular attention to leaving your arms relaxed and NOT doing a reverse curl to get the bar to your shoulders. Allow your hip drive send it right up your torso to your shoulders. Remember that <u>your arms are NOT used to bring the bar upward but to pull you down under the bar.</u>

Here we go:
1. Start by standing straight with a wooden dowel (or PVC "rattle stick") using the Clean grip.
2. Tilt over slightly and bend your knees, keeping the bar against your upper thighs (Launch Point for the Clean), your torso straight and your weight on your heels, and your feet slightly closer than hip width (or in your established set position stance, if you're a veteran lifter)
3. Holding the bar against your upper thighs and with your back straight, stick your tailbone out to the rear until your forefeet come off the floor. During this phase, your torso should tilt over (back remains straight) and your legs will straighten somewhat. Do NOT go to locked knees here.
4. Then, bring your hips forward, causing the feet to return to the floor, and raise your torso quickly.
5. At the instant the front of your feet touch the floor and with your balance still over the rear of your feet, explosively drive the hips upwards and inwards, catapulting the bar upwards, bring the torso to vertical and drive the bar to your shoulders, now using your traps and arms (elbow bend upwards, then rotate around the bar) to pull yourself down slightly to the high receiving position (Power) with slightly bent knees.
6. "Catch" the bar in the groove <u>behind</u> your front deltoids and crossing your collarbones, with bent knees and flat feet (balance mid-foot), now shuffled out slightly wider than they started and chest pointing forward. (By the way, on your way through this movement, you have now performed a Power Clean from a very high hanging position.)
7. Now, bring the bar down, return to the starting position and do it again and again and again. Do three to four sets of ten.

Rock & Roll Power Clean

Doing the Clean version of the Rock & Roll is a bit harder than the Snatch to me because there is more of a tendency to try to muscle the bar. Remember to let the hips do it.

Part B

Below are the steps for combining the first and second pull drills to give you a rudimentary Power Clean.

Use a dowel or a very light tech bar. Practice some Clean Grip Rock & Rolls. Pause for a second in the middle of that drill when the front of your feet have returned to the platform and, then finishing the movement. Use the DVD extensively throughout this portion of the process as a guide.

Here we go again:

1. Take the correct Clean Set position.
2. Do a Partial Deadlift/Sweep and STOP as the bar reaches a launch point on the thighs, keeping your feet flat and staying "through the heels".
3. From that position, SHIFT your torso upward and your knees forward (scoop) and catapult the bar to the correct position on your shoulders for the Power Clean.
4. Reset your feet and do it again, trying not to pause at the Launch Point.
5. Repeat this couplet (one stopping and one not)
6. Do this drill in sets of five to ten couplets.

Basic Power Clean

By combining the Partial Deadlift and Sweep through the 1st pull, shifting position and then performing the explosive catapulting portion of the Rock and Roll drill during the 2nd pull, you will be doing a basic Power Clean. This lift is probably the most used Olympic lift by athletes in all sports. Perfect it.

After you master this combination of drills, start doing only the whole bottom to top drill (Set to Receiving position) without stopping at all. After you advance to this point, don't slow down until the bar is on your shoulders. By now you should be performing a pretty good, basic Power Clean.

Again, I suggest that you watch the DVD before doing this step.

Step 10: The Full Squat Clean from the Launch Point

First, warm up for this by doing two to three sets of Air Squats with your hands behind your head. Then, move on to do a couple of sets of Front Squats (full squat with bar across your collarbones and hands in Clean grip) with light weight and pause at the bottom position a few times. And, finally move on to doing some Rock & Rolls with the Clean grip.

Full Squat Clean from the Launch Point:

1. Do 2 Clean grip R & R's and at the receiving position sit down through flat feet to full depth Front Squat.
2. Do several sets of this, only stopping momentarily before going into the Front Squat. You must emphasize sitting down through your heels when descending into the Front Squat.
3. If you accomplish this and can go down to at least a parallel squat, start attempting to eliminate the pause and go right into the squat after completing the Rock & Roll movement to the shoulders.
4. Do several sets of three to five repetitions, if this movement is successful.
5. Now, stop the R&R when your feet return to the flat position after being balanced on your heels. Count to 3. Complete the rest of the R&R movement and continue to the full Clean position.

Launch Point to Full Clean

Two or three times through this sequence should produce a reasonable Squat Clean for most, at least from a hip high starting position. If you are having real trouble getting into any reasonable squat position and you also had great difficulty doing the Overheads and the Drops earlier in the book, you may have to use the Split Style Clean, if you want to get to any position lower than your Power (high) receiving position. That position is demonstrated on the DVD, as is the Split Snatch position for those of you (us) who can't achieve a good, low squat in either or one of the lifts.

Full Squat Clean from the Hang

This may be the hardest lift in this section. Not because you can't squat or don't know how to catapult a weight by now, but because of the starting position and the movements immediately at the start of this lift.

1. Lower the bar, still gripping it with your Clean grip, to your knees.
2. Set your shoulders in exactly the position they would be in if you were starting the bar from the floor. (directly over the bar)
3. Start the movement by sweeping the bar inward and moving your knees back, just as you would from the floor and allow your back to tilt over, keeping the bar swept in.
4. Drive towards the Launch Point and allow your knees to come forward as you raise your back. (scoop)
5. Catapult the bar from the Launch Point to the Power Clean position on your shoulders.
6. Pause for a moment, if you have to, and then go into a full squat Clean position.
7. Do the lift from the knees again and try to eliminate the Pause at the top.

Squat Clean from Hang

The hard part is making yourself go through the movements that you would from the floor, when the bar is in a hanging position. Your brain will tell you to simply fire upward from the point at which the bar is hanging. This is wrong, as I discussed earlier. <u>You must put the legs, hips and back through the same sequence of movements they will go through when lifting a bar from the floor, when doing a hang from anywhere below the Launch Point.</u>

CHAPTER III: The Ten-Step Method   117

Watch the DVD for a visual on this lift. Again, it is better than written or spoken words.

The Full Squat Clean from the Floor

This can be even more difficult than from the hip or knee but, if you have completed the Rock & Roll drill (2nd pull) and the Partial Deadlift/Sweep drill (1st pull), it should not be that hard to go on to a Full Squat Clean from the floor.
Here we go.

1. Do the Partial Dead./Sweep from the Set position to the Launch Point.
2. Now, continue through the Rock & Roll (flat-footed version) without stopping and to the receiving position of your basic Power Clean.
3. Do this for several sets of 3-5.
4. Again, do a Front Squat after "catching" the Power Clean with only a minimal hesitation.
5. Then, try again to go to the squat without any hesitation at the top.

Squat Clean from Floor

If you can't accomplish this, take your time, do a few Front Squats and try again to work through this sequence. If it is really difficult for you to come close to getting reasonable positions, you may have to try the Split positions I spoke of earlier, until it is easier for you to go to the squat position. They're on the DVD.

If you've worked on these last two drills for an hour or so, it's time for a break. You may even want to come back fresh tomorrow and try them again. They will click.

You should now have fairly good, basic form in the major Olympic-style lifts. It may take another two or three sessions for everything to click. It is not easy and it does not all come at once. You will have ups and downs in both of these lifts at different times. But, if you keep to the basic ideas I've presented to you about form and you read this book and keep the ideas about why we use these techniques, it will come to you. And, keep referring back to the DVD. There is nothing anyone can write or say that will "explain" these lifts as well as you watching people do them correctly.

A Quick Word about the Split Style

Whether receiving the bar in the Split-style Power (high) or the Full Split (low), the basics of it are the same. Your legs are split to the front and back, much like the Split Jerk. They do not end up in a straight line (tightrope) but should be straight back and forward of their starting positions. In fact, catching a "Split" high looks much like a Jerk, as far as leg position. The big difference between the Split for catching a Clean or a Snatch and splitting for a Jerk is balance on the feet, use of the back leg and position of the knee over the front of the foot. The big difference in the Power Split and the Full Split is that in the Full Split the legs simply end up further apart in the Full Split, with the back leg straighter and the front knee further in front of the front foot.

The balance during the Split Clean or Snatch is more on the front leg. The back leg is driven backward and down and is more for balance than for support. The knee of the front leg, as you go lower is allowed to go out in front of the knee (unlike the correct positioning in the Split Jerk). However, there is a basic weakness in the position because 1) recovery is done on more or less one leg and 2) the bar is always pulled a bit more in front of the lifter in this style than the squat style.

However, if you really can't get into the squat position quickly, this is a great way to perform the lifts. Many athletes have done tremendous lifting using this receiving style. This is a good Power Clean style for those of you who might be larger athletes, such as football linemen. You can do the Power (high) versions of the lifts in very quick fashion, saving a lot of total training time and, since the manner of receiving the bar is not critical for most sports, the split-style is still used by many.

I suggest you vary your front foot in the split, if you are playing sports other than Olympic weightlifting. As in the Split Jerk, alternating between left and right leg leads makes you more balanced and agile. However, if you are performing near maximum lifts, I would suggest using whichever leg relationship is more natural for you.

It is a time for a break from training.

ROADSIDE ATTRACTION
ATHLETES, RATE YOUR TRAINING PROGRAM
(WOT* or PDG*)
*Waste of Time or *Pretty Damn Good

1. Spending more time using machines than free weights (dumbbells, barbells)---WOT
2. Not doing Olympic-style lifts or variations---WOT
3. Doing Olympic-style lifts with improper form---WOT
4. Doing many exercises to FAILURE---WOT (teaches you to FAIL)
5. Never squatting---WOT
6. Never squatting below parallel---WOT
7. Using a lot of wobbly boards or bouncy balls---WOT
8. Using predominantly "free weights" in program---PDG
9. Doing Olympic-style lifts or variations with proper form---PDG
10. Varying volume and intensity and seldom FAIL in workouts---PDG (success breeds success)
11. Doing squats below parallel---PDG

I can't guarantee that if your strength and conditioning program includes 8-11 that it will be successful, but at least it's headed in the right direction. Listen to your coach. He is trying to do a good job.

I can guarentee, however, that if your strength program falls into the 1-7 category, it's a WOT.
Many programs run by individual team coaches around the country try to fill a need for power/ speed/quickness, by offering plyometrics, agility, some functional strength or core work. There is often some gymnastic or speed work, as well. These exercises can help you gain some strength and increase your power potential. These programs are often built on good intentions and good sense and are sometimes put in place because there isn't the time, money or space available for more. This won't replace a program built around a core of Olympic-style lifts, but any sound, partial program is better than no program at all in the short term.

However, any program designed for developing truly powerful athletes that overlooks the major strength/power exercises is futile in the long run. Plyos and the rest may make up the top of the athletic pyramid. The base and most of the body of the pyramid that will make huge differences in strength and the ability to produce power are the Olympic-style lifts, full (below parallel) squats, deadlifts, jerks and pulls (drives).

I want to talk about two aspects of training here, as long as we're taking a break from the road.

COACHES: There are some specific uses for partial squats, but to use them as the major squat technique used in a program is ludicrous. The vast majority of those who are proponents of parallel or above parallel squatting are ill informed and are preventing athletes from reaching their potential. A major cause of non-contact knee injury -ACL, torn cartilage, ravaged meniscus-and lower back injuries is doing too many of these parallel and above parallel squats, which do not strengthen the legs and hips properly. Partial and parallel squats are arguably more damaging than no squats at all. Let me explain quickly.

Partial (above parallel) squats have little strengthening affect for any other movement than themselves. They bring undo pressure on the spine because the limited range of motion involved increases the load that athletes will use too quickly. Athletes will not be totally strengthened through the range of motion of the muscles involved, creating a top-heavy structure with no foundation. There is little to say, except in very particular cases, for the application of this exercise. There is no general use in athletics for this exercise.

Parallel squats put athletes in one of the weakest positions found in weightlifting and expect them to deal with the top load they will likely have to lift in the training program. Because the thigh is parallel to the floor, the quadriceps are stretched and the back is tipped forward for balance with the load on the athletes shoulders. The load is now as far forward of the fulcrum at the hips as it can be before the structural collapse of the entire system.

In order to ascend from this precarious position, extreme pressure is put on the knees as the quads try to extend that joint to rise up. Also, undo pressure is exerted on the lower back because of the angle of the back. Shearing pressure is present at the knee joint because of the extreme angle of the torso. The glutes and hamstrings can't help efficiently in ascending because of this overall position. All in all, it is an accident waiting to happen.

By the way: Unless you plan to compete during earthquakes, there is no use doing major work on wobbly platforms of any kind.

Good Squat   *Bad Squat*   *Useless Squat*

Chapter IV: Over Your Head

The Split Jerk, the Power Jerk and the Squat Jerk

The Jerk is the lift in which the bar goes from a groove crossing the collarbones and shoulders to arms length overhead with a single, powerful thrust from the hips and legs and a fast punch upwards from the arms. In the sport of Olympic Weightlifting, it is the final part of what is called the "King of Lifts": the Clean and Jerk, which is the heaviest overhead lift done by competitors and is widely considered the true measure of a lifter's power and strength. Taking a bit of liberty with that analogy, you might consider the Jerk to be the Crown on top of the King's head.

Whether you split your legs front and back (Split Jerk), shuffle them a bit to the sides (Power Jerk) or even descend into a squat position (Squat Jerk) to catch the Jerk makes no difference in how you perform the dip and drive phase of the lift. You Clean or Power Clean the bar to your shoulders, dip your torso straight down and then drive your hips and legs upward and accelerate the bar overhead. You remember the drill to teach you the basics of this back in the "Up against the Wall" section, earlier in the pre-drills. You then move your feet to the proper catch position while thrusting your shoulders and arms upward against the bar explosively, which will actually push you downward away from the bar.

The Squat Jerk requires you to have very good flexibility in all major joints and extremely good balance. The potential for lifting more absolute weight is there for you, if you can easily go to a full squat immediately after driving the bar in the Jerk. This lift is not very stable in comparison to the other two styles. I would not use this style for athletes in sports other than Olympic Weightlifting. Even if you compete in that sport, I don't believe it is a technique to be taught to or tried by beginners or even many lifters who are serious competitors. It is important to note that it is a very successful style for lifting a great amount of weight overhead by those who are good at it.

Split Jerk

Some Thoughts About the Split Jerk
(Force Direction and Foot Positions)

It is important to understand that the Jerk is essentially a down-up-down movement done mostly through the heels. You rise to your forefeet to follow through and to split your legs to the front and rear at the finish. The hip and leg drive rams the bar from the shoulders towards arm's length. As it rises, your arms drive you downward and your feet seek the platform. The split should not be considered a conscious lunge.

For the Jerk, the bar should be in a groove running over your collarbones and behind the front deltoids. The dip and drive is the emphasis, not the nuances of the split. Foot position in the split is important. But, if it is too structured and emphasized in your mind, you will try to go to the split before you've finished driving the bar in an effort to make the perfect split. That will limit what you actually lift.

I am going to teach you this lift from the Dip and Drive to the Recovery from the Split. You should learn the Jerk as completely separate lift from the other overhead movements that start with the bar on the shoulders. Those lifts are slow and the Jerk is lightning fast. Relating the movements of these slower movements too strongly to it does not set a good foundation for learning the correct muscle use sequence or the rhythm of the Jerk.

The Split's Not Simple…But It's Easy

The Split Jerk looks simple until you get a bar on your shoulders and try to do it. The following, purposely run-on sentence explaining Jerk technique, will give you an idea why:

You stand straight with your feet at a slightly closer than hip width and with the bar resting on your clavicles and dip your hips downward, descending over your heels and keeping your torso erect down toward and up away from the low point of the dip, which is several inches downward, you drive your hips upward, at first staying through your heels, and then, as the accelerating bar leaves your shoulders you continue upward, onto the balls of your feet and split your legs forward and back and reach upward with your arms in a punching fashion, driving yourself downward away from the bar to a landing position in which the front foot is flat on the ground and may be turned slightly inwards with the shin extending upwards vertically from it, while the rear foot lands first, and on the ball of the foot with the foot in plantar flexion and the knee of the rear leg slightly bent while the bar is, at the same instant, overhead and at arms length, vertically over the rear portion of your head.

Geeeessshh, are you kidding! If it were that simple, we wouldn't see it missed so much in Olympic weightlifting competitions.

Your confusion while reading the above explanation is minor when compared to attempting to actually perform a split jerk correctly in the real world in a fraction of a second with a bar loaded with weight pressing down on your shoulders. Your brain is confused at first because of the different planes through which the upper an lower body have to move at different times during the Jerk.

Because of prior experience you will tend to tense your hands, arms and shoulders when you are holding the bar, rather than relaxing them as is necessary at the start of the Jerk. Throw in the idea or putting a massive weight above your head and the brain is not a happy camper. Add to this the fact that your archenemy in weightlifting, <u>common sense</u>, is telling you that you have to lunge forward and under that bar on your shoulders if you want it to end up over your head and you get a glimpse of the problems with this lift.
I think I can help.

Staying Sane and Simplifying the Jerk Split
(First, Take a Short Walk)

A step, in fact, will do. Start with your feet even and a normal distance apart. Step forward with whichever foot seems most natural to lead. Stop the forward leg when the back edge of the heel touches the ground. Then, slowly put the rest of that foot down, allowing that knee to bend. Keep the balance of that forward leg on the heel and continue to bend the knee until the shin is vertical.

You will notice that while you have been doing all this work on your front foot, your rear foot has placed itself on its front half and has done a nice plantar flexion. The knee of the rear leg has also bent slightly. Now, turn your front foot slightly inwards. Voila! You have created a perfectly good split.

One-step Split Jerk

The Drive: The Jerk in the Box

Start by reviewing the "Up against the Wall" drill on page 60. Do it again, for two or three sets.

Next, draw a 3' by 3' square with chalk in the middle of your lifting platform. Then draw a line across it, side to side, at about one foot from the front edge. Now, draw two lines down the middle from the front to the back of the square about 6-8" apart. It should look like the picture below:

This is the box in which you are going to start to learn the Jerk. Since I believe that the Jerk should be taught as primarily a down-up-down movement, I am going to have you line up with your toes touching that line across the Box and I am going to insist that you not split front or back to any distance that would put either of your feet outside the margins of the Box. My purpose here is to teach you the idea of splitting to only the distance needed rather than splitting wide for any jerk. Don't put your feet inside the two lines in the middle of the square going from the front to the back. This is simply to keep the side-to-side base of support broader. If your feet came close to being in line, it would be like split jerking on a balance beam or a high wire. If anything, you want your feet to veer away from the centerline slightly in order to widen your base of support.

The Jerk Box

So, the first rules are:

1) All splits will be inside the Box.
2) At no time will you have your feet between the front-back lines.

Start the drills standing in the Box with your toes touching the line at 2' and your <u>hands on your hips or out to the sides for balance</u>.

Here's the drill:

1. Stand straight, feet pointed slightly outward, with your balance over your heels.
2. Tighten your abs and take a breath
3. Dip for four to six inches through the heels, keeping your torso vertical

4. You should start the drive upward through your heels, and as you drive up onto the balls of your feet, split forward and back, taking as short a step forward and back as possible.
5. You should land with your front foot down flat and turned in slightly, your front shin vertical, and your back foot flexed and the rear leg slightly bent at the knee.
6. You should do 5-8 repetitions with the goal of achieving the shortest, fastest, correct split possible

Work that split

Off the top of my head-Jerk

Get to a correct split in which the front foot is only a few inches forward of the back foot. If you think of trying to get the heel of your front foot to land first, you will usually land flat-footed, which is correct. Do the drill again <u>with your hands clasped behind your head.</u> Keep trying for that shortest, fastest split jerk stance.

Now, <u>do the drill again with a dowel, held up lightly with the clean grip, on top of your head</u>, over the back of your ears. Follow through and Jerk the bar to arms length when you drive upwards and go into your split. Make sure that your split is short and that the bar is at arms length and your scapulae-shoulder blades-are pressed together as your feet touch down on the platform in a correct split relationship.

WARNING! WARNING! WARNING! WARNING! WARNING!

NEVER do that drill with anything but a 5-6' PVC or wooden dowel on your head. Using a weightlifting bar will only lead to bumps and a sore neck. Do this drill for five to eight repetitions.

During the next section, where you will learn more about the dip and drive, keep using the Box when you are doing your drills. Keep emphasizing what you learned in this section and pretty soon the Box will not be needed as a guide and you will be jerking better than most. Eventually, you will be jerking a weight that requires a longer split than the three-foot distance but not for some time and you will be ready for it when that time comes.

Learning the Dip and Drive: What to Emphasize

The foundation of having a good Jerk, no matter what the foot and body position at the catch, is having a good dip and drive phase. If you don't have this, I don't care if your split, power or squat position looks like it should be in the Louvre, you won't jerk a thing.

First, put the bar on the front of your shoulders correctly. Your shoulders are forward of neutral, at this stage.

Here's the set-up:

1. The bar should be resting behind the front deltoids and across the collarbones.
2. Stand straight, feet angled slightly outward, with your weight balanced over your heels.
3. Elbows should be pointed downwards (45 deg or more) and slightly outward.
4. The bar should be in the your palms somewhere, not in your fingers.
5. Tighten your abs and take a breath in before starting the dip.
6. Make sure your legs are straight but relaxed before starting the dip.
7. Look forward and slightly upward before the dip.
8. You may pull the chin inwards before starting the dip.
9. Relax your hands and arms before and during the dip.

As you begin the dip & drive, 1) dip straight downward through your heels and 2) <u>allow</u> your knees forward to dip rather than forcibly flexing them. Learn to do these two things only, and your jerk will improve.

Here's the whole movement:

1. <u>Allow</u> your knees to move forward and start to descend, keeping your hips over your heels (or slightly behind) and keeping your torso vertical.
2. As you reach the bottom of the dip of 3-6," brake the descent by tightening the glutes, hams.
3. Start the drive upwards though your heels (not the front of your feet) using explosive hip and knee extension.
4. As the drive proceeds, go onto the balls of your feet, completing the hip extension and then to move to the catch position (split or power position).
5. Your torso has remained vertical throughout and your shoulders and hands should be relaxed.

6. <u>AFTER</u> the bar has been driven from the shoulders by this explosive hip and knee extension, elbow extension will occur and your shoulders will reach upward until the arms are straight and are supporting the bar overhead. The shoulder and arm "punch" is actually moving you downward away from the bar as the split is taking place.
7. The position of the bar overhead should be vertically over the back of your head.

Dip and Drive to Split Jerk

A critical point to remember when performing the jerk is to <u>NOT</u> raise your shoulders to assist with driving the bar from the torso. Raising the shoulders before the bar leaves the torso only removes the bar from the solid base of your skeleton and causes you to tense up as your trapezius muscles try to lift the shoulders with a weight on top of them. This will, in turn, cause premature tension in the muscles of the arms and over-arching of the back. More often than not, it also leads to the bar being driven forward rather than to a proper position over the back of the head. It can also result in you hitting yourself in the chin with the bar. This idea of raising of your shoulders to help lift the bar off the torso is still in many texts. It is wrong. Rip out the pages proposing this technique, if you are going to keep the book.

Now, back to the lift.

Your torso will remain vertical and along with your hips will move slightly forward as the split occurs. <u>Your back foot reaches the platform before the front foot when splitting</u> because the back leg is longer than the front when both are flexed for the correct split positioning and simply reaches the floor first. Because of this, it pushes your hips forward a bit in a correct Jerk.

However, believe that you are keeping your torso in the same place during the split. This will help you to think of only driving the bar and lessens the tendency to lunge forward during the jerk to help yourself get under the bar which is simply wrong. Do this lift as if your torso is inside a wall. That way, you're more likely to descend, drive and descend again with your torso still in a vertical alignment. Getting the bar overhead to the correct position will occur if you drive it well.

Remember the rule that applies to every sports movement when learning the Jerk. These movements all start more slowly than they finish. Don't dip more quickly than you can drive back upward. You will find that gravity provides enough quickness during the descent and you don't have to try to add to it. <u>Allow</u> your knees to move forward rather than forcibly flex them forward to start the dip. If you start the dip too quickly you'll leave the bar in mid air above your shoulders, be forced onto the balls of your feet, or worse yet, have your torsos tilt forward because of the excessive speed of descent. All of these flaws will limit your ability to jerk well.

You should also learn to quickly squeeze your scapulae together at the final overhead catch position of the jerk. This will help the muscles of the torso support the bar above the head, taking pressure off the shoulders. And, it will insure that the vertical positioning of the bar will be correct. When the bar is jerked, it moves up and back. Its final position should be directly over your shoulders, which have been pressed back and up. Your shoulder blades, pressed together, help support the bar position overhead.

A Little Trick to Stop Tipping when Dipping

You may find that you are dipping through the front of your feet instead of through the heels when doing Jerks. This will cause your torso to tip forward. And, it leads to difficult, forward or off-balanced jerks. This habit may occur with only the foot of the front leg in the split or with both feet. The cause of this is usually that you are rushing onto the balls of the feet to get to the split in too much of a hurry. The Drive, of course, will suffer. In the split jerk, you should only be on the balls of your feet near the top of the drive as you start the movement downwards and to the front and back for the split. So, how do you fix this?

The simple trick of lifting your big toe to the inside top of your shoe or shoes at the start of the dip can fix this flaw. Don't consciously try to keep it there throughout but just do it before you dip and as you descend. The rest will usually take care of itself and you should learn that you are supposed to dip through your heels and start upwards through them as well. Some coaches seem to be teaching their athletes to start the jerk by lifting the entire front of their feet off the floor just before the dip and then putting them down at the bottom of the dip. Don't do this. It does not work well and can lead to the Jerk being pushed too far forward.

As I said above, I believe it is crucial that you learn that the Jerk is basically a down-up-down movement. Your hips and legs control this lift and are the primary movers here, with hip extension, again, taking the forefront. Your torso is a virtual battering ram that is driven upwards by them, delivering force to the bar, which is on your shoulders, and collarbones. Your legs split forward and back only to achieve a stable, slightly lower catch position that increases your base of support. Your legs should split only as much as necessary with no predetermined step length to the front or rear.

Your feet should go directly forward and back when splitting or veer slightly wider from the positions they are in at the start, which should be under your hips or slightly narrower. You should never look like your feet are on a tightrope at the finish of a split. Your front foot should be turned inward slightly when it lands and the balance on that foot should be toward the mid to rear foot. Your front shinbone should always be vertical at the finish of the split or slightly angled towards you.

Your rear leg in a split should <u>NOT</u> be thrust backward in a more or less horizontal line, like that of a shot-putter, but is to be thrust <u>downward</u> seeking the platform. It should be driven directly back from its starting point (or slightly outside that line). There should be a slight bend at the knee of the rear leg. The foot of your rear leg should be supported on its forefoot only (plantar flexed). The distance between your front foot and the back will be greater as the weight on the bar gets heavier and youaren't able to drive it as high. It should reach the platform an instant before the front foot, pushing the hips forward slightly.

Remember, this forward leg and foot position is used as a brace and along with your back leg brace and the musculature around your hips is creating a strong pyramid that is the foundation for your torso, which should be held vertical. All this is to offer support for the bar, which should be positioned at arm's length, over the back of your head, directly above your shoulders. Simple, huh.

At the finish of the split, your hip musculature should tighten to stop the descent of your torso. This should happen at the same time your feet get positioned on the platform. Many lifters emphasize using the quadriceps to solidify this position. The quads of both legs do help solidify the base of the lifter in this position but the real tightening should be felt around your hips, mostly in the glutes and hamstrings. Overemphasis of tightening your quads can bring about excessive knee flexion, which will weaken the split's supportive nature.

The proper emphasis on the dip and drive brings about splits of varying distances, depending on the weight on the bar: light weight-small split, heavier weight-longer split. But, certain rules do remain in all of these splits.

1. Your front foot always moves forward of its starting position.
2. Your back foot always moves backward from its starting position and reaches down to the floor an instant before your front foot.
3. Your front shin is always vertical or angled slightly back towards the lifter in the split.
4. Your back leg is always slightly bent at the knee in the split.
5. Your front foot is turned slightly inwards and lands flat-seemingly heel first.
6. Your back foot is pointed straight forward and lands on its front half, but never the toes.
7. Your feet never move towards the centerline of your body.
8. Your feet move straight forward and back (or slightly away from your centerline) from their starting position.
9. Your starting position for the feet should be under your hips or slightly narrower .for most.

10. Your torso should remain vertical throughout the lift.
11. You should control the finish of the lift, as your feet hit the platform, from the hips.

Recovery from the Split Jerk Stance

Once the bar is overhead and at arm's length, your next chore is to recover to a more stable position and get ready to put the bar back down on the floor. You should learn to go to the position that Olympic weightlifters use for their final stance in this lift, which is placing your feet about shoulder width apart lined up with each other across the frontal plane, with the bar still at arm's length overhead also lined up with the frontal plane.

But how do you get there from the split?

Here's the technique, step by step:

1. Using a controlled knee extension of the front leg, push back through your heel and take a backwards step of about your foot length, keeping the rear foot in place for a stable brace.
2. Repeat this motion once more and when the front foot is again flat on the floor, bring your back foot up to a position in the same plane as the front and about shoulder distance away from it.

This process will tend to keep the bar from gaining too much momentum forward or back as you recover to a normal standing position and it allows you to be in as much control as possible, given the nature of the movement needed. Straighten your legs but don't bring your feet together when finishing the recovery from the Split Jerk. It creates an unstable structure that resembles an upside-down pyramid.

In recovering from the Power or Squat versions of the Jerk, little foot movement is needed. You should simply stand up to straight legs. That makes the recovery from these techniques relatively easy.

Athletes: Most of you should learn to do the split with either foot forward and back. This makes it a more valuable training exercise for you and prevents natural imbalances from becoming a bigger problem. In fact, it helps you to become more powerful pushing off either leg. This goes for CrossFitters as well.

Let's take a break over there.

*****

Roadside Attraction
(Earth shattering revelations about weightlifting, etc.)

1. Olympic weightlifting is gymnastics with a bar in your hands.
2. The biggest challenge in learning the Olympic-style lifts is teaching your gross motor muscles to be as agile as your fine motor muscles.
3. The second biggest challenge in learning the Olympic-style lifts is teaching yourself to use the muscles you can't see as easily as you use the muscles you can.
4. Don't look down.
5. There's no such thing as a flat-assed athlete.
6. Performing an Olympic lift is like taking your hand off a hot frying pan: if you think, you get burned.
7. If you need quiet to train for your sport, play golf.
8. Bench pressing is important for football players because when guys that do the Olympic lifts pancake them, they can lift them off their chests.
9. You don't jump to drive the bar upwards in Olympic Weightlifting..
10. The human body did NOT evolve to play sports.
11. The only thing lifting to failure is good for is teaching lifters to fail.
12. Coaching weightlifting is not rocket science but it is a science.
13. There is only one test for a coach and it ain't on paper.
14. If you can't "see" it, you'll never be able to teach it.
15. If you want to be a better athlete, trust someone else to teach you how to do things better.

16. Coaching = Science (one part) + Art (two parts)
17. If you want to be a better athlete? Look, listen and ask.
18. If you want to be a better coach? Look, listen and ask.
19. The best athletes love the stage. The worst athletes love to sit in the audience.
20. Competitive sport is a test of physical skill, not a measure of physical fitness.
21. In weightlifting, the glutes run the show.

*****

Rest Stop for Strength Coaches
(A general guide)

Two classic mistakes in teaching the Olympic-style lifts to athletes is to have them 1) emphasize a conscious, aggressive knee extension in the 2nd pull and 2) to have them elevate their shoulders during the 2nd pull by contracting their trapezius upward. These actions will combine to move the athletes and the bar too far forward as they rise and will slow and misdirect their transition to the 3rd pull.

It is essential at this point to minimize the time the feet are actually off the floor or even pushing upwards. By actively jumping upwards into the air, driving into an extreme plantar flexion or even by simply not actively accelerating themselves downward at this point, the athletes are making a crucial technical error. This error causes them to not maximize the rate of change in the relationship between them and the bar by direction and velocity. The outcome will often be that the athletes and the bar arrive at the catch position at approximately the same time, going in the same direction. DOWN! This will generally lead to one or two bad situations. (1) The bar cannot be racked properly and pulls them forward and downward or (2) the bar cannot be shouldered whatsoever (or held overhead, in the case of a snatch) and simply falls to the floor.

The correct technique is as follows. As the second pull ends, with a dominant hip extension and assisting knee extension, the feet should engage in shuffling quickly out from the pulling position stance towards a wider catch position stance. The height reached by plantar flexion (rising onto the balls of the feet), which will occur with most lifters who have explosively extended their hips, should be minimized and lifters should be taught to drive their feet toward the stance they will need to receive the bar in the squat or higher Power position. It should also be emphasized to the lifters to get their heels back to the surface as quickly as possible at this point.

Shuffling or barely lifting the feet to the outside is also important for most to achieve a wider based catch position that is stable, quickly completed and them to keep their torsos relatively upright at the receiving position. Encourage athletes to land flatfooted, with feet about at hip width (for most). Many international Olympic weightlifters now barely lift their feet at all, trying rather to stay in contact with the platform so that they can deliver force more efficiently for a longer period of time throughout the movement. This should be the model.

Here are some simple guidelines.

1. Tell athletes to get their heels back in touch with the platform as soon as possible after they finish the 2nd pull.

2. Tell athletes that they should be thinking that they are pulling their hips down to the final catch position, not their shoulders.

3. Do not allow athletes to go to a wider receiving stance as the weight on the bar gets heavier and isn't driven as high. Rather, have them catch at a lower hip position with the same receiving stance.

Usually, team sport athletes have a hard time learning to land flatfooted at first because so much of their experience has taught them to be on their forefeet when playing their sport. It is good to remind them that the flatfooted stance with their butts back a bit is better for catching these lifts because it balances the weight of the bar in front of them.

Constantly catching of Olympic lifts on the forefeet or with too wide a stance or both will take a toll on the knees, elbows and backs of athletes. <u>It is not the lifts that are causing the injuries. It is incorrect technique.</u>

Chapter V: Man as a Machine

The Human Lifting Machine: Catapults, Cranes, Pendulums and Slingshots

"Humans did not evolve solely to lift weights." - Don McCauley

I know some of my follow weightlifting coaches might not want to accept the above statement, but unless someone starts unearthing barbell sets in the caves of Neanderthals or the digs along the Great Rift in Africa, I'll stand by that statement.

However, when presented with the task of lifting weights at great speed, to their shoulders or overhead in competition, humans do what they have always done best. They problem solve. They tinker and think and tinker and think until they find the best way to accomplish the task. And, as in most physical tasks, humans find the best answers by looking at the tools they've invented to do the work they can't physically do on their own. Many times they find that they can substantially imitate one or several of these tools -or machines- to create a sublime, rhythmic, athletic movement that is—well—human.

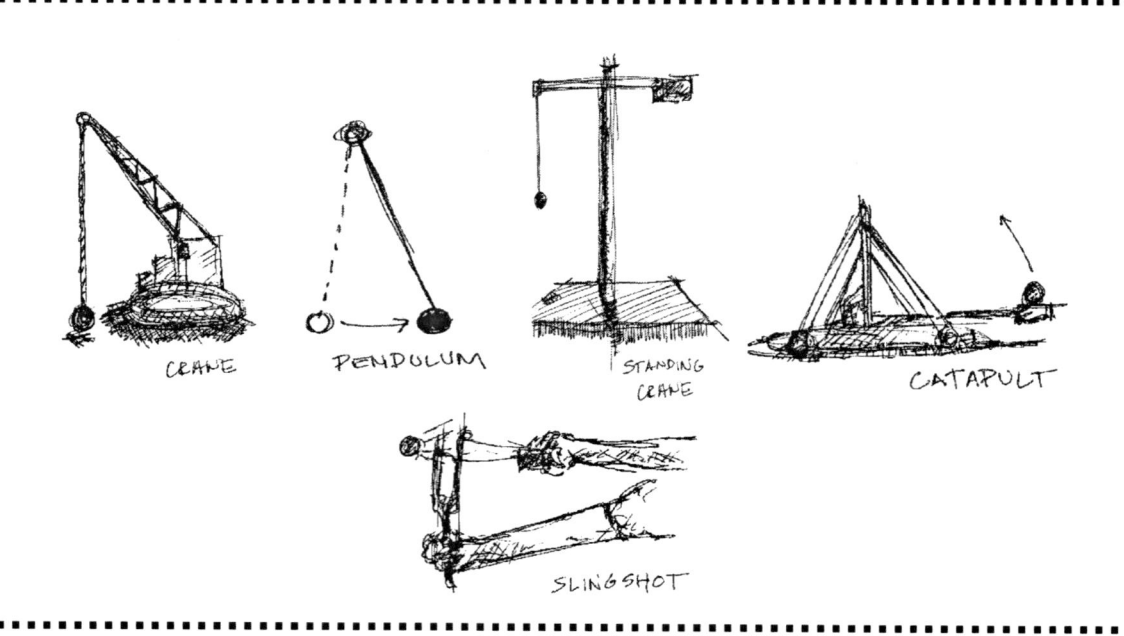

The Cranes and the Pendulum
(The machines of the First Pull)

When a person first sees the Olympic-style lifts being performed, his eyes often misinterpret what they see. His brain tries to relate it to how, in his own experiences, he has tried to lift objects to shoulder height or above. When he first tries these lifts, things get pretty ugly pretty fast. The back is rounded, the arms are bent and the bar either doesn't move much or is sent on a course toward the next county, not towards the shoulders or overhead. Occasionally, with great effort, the novice hoists the bar to his shoulders, but seldom has a satisfied look on his face. His brain usually can't comprehend how the little girl he just saw do the same weight lifted it so effortlessly. First, the novice lifter's brain has to be taught what it is seeing. Often, this is a long process, given that the brain often learns through prior experience and the movements that accomplish these Olympic-style lifts are not often part of people's physical action memory.

What the brain is actually seeing is the lifter mimicking several machines, melding their actions in seamless transition. With the use of some unique weightlifting tricks, athletes accomplish the task of moving the bar from the floor to their shoulders or overhead in an explosive and exciting manner. The following is what is happening and why.

During the 1st pull the athlete takes his Set position; he should mimic the look of a standard harbor crane. These giants are typically lined up along the edges of the dock areas of ports around the world, looking like so many silent, steel Godzillas, contemplating what to smash in downtown Tokyo. Their major function, however, is to off-load container ships. They also, coincidentally, provide weightlifters a good idea about what his most advantageous position might be to start lifting heavy bars from the floor.

Setting the center of his mass nearer the floor, his back in angled only slightly and his shoulders directly over the load to be lifted, is a strong Set position for the lifter. A human lifter doesn't have steel wires running through his shoulders down to the load and no motor to rewind the wire to lift the load. To compensate, the human machine shifts his weight on his feet from the front to the back and along with a subtle bit of help from his back (lats), he creates an inward pendulum movement of his arms and the load they are lifting. *Cranes everywhere envy this very human ability.* This essential movement brings the center of mass of the load closer to the lifter's center of mass while they both rise.

Now that the load and the lifter are rising, the lifter must morph into another type of crane familiar to us all. Humans in this part of the journey imitate the Tower Crane we see, it seems, in every city.

As he nears the next phase of the Olympic lift, he starts to tilt over to the front. Like the tower crane, the lifter's counterbalanced by a heavy load-his Center of Mass (COM) as the weight being lifted comes upward and inward. The pendulum reaches its innermost point and suddenly-SCOOP! The lifter becomes a Catapult.

The change is immediate and necessary because the human lifter is 1) at is most precarious position in the 1st pull and 2) he is about to drive the bar higher than the top of the crane—the shoulders. The Catapult is a good choice for this task. It can drive projectiles to greater heights than itself by simply uncoiling. In Olympic-style lifting, humans only need to drive the bar a small, vertical distance by extending. And, once the lifter has performed the scoop, he has positioned his hips in such a way that he only has to release them correctly to drive the projectile (the bar) higher.

Positioning, Loading and Firing the Catapult
(The double knee bend revisited)

At this point in their task of lifting a bar on top of the shoulders or overhead quickly, humans resort to another little trick. The <u>double knee bend</u> or <u>scoop</u> lowers the hips, while also slightly extending them and puts lifters in a better position to deliver force to the bar.

The repositioned body is now coiled and ready to strike with great force as it reaches the bar at the Launch Point, which is now closer to the hip joint and the hip extensors. This positioning of bar and body allows lifters to perform an extremely powerful hip extension upwards while grounded and balanced over their base of support. From the back of the feet, the hips extend upward and only slightly forward. With the conscious delivery of the tremendous force of hip extension, the bar is driven almost vertically into the air.

The human machine has now positioned, loaded and unleashed its Catapult. The force of the hip extension, which should be delivered in as vertical direction as possible, will force the heels of the lifter up and the human form will force him forward slightly on his feet. This human catapult endeavors to remain grounded when he delivers force, and on as solid a base as possible.

If the lifter puts emphasis early in this phase on consciously driving high onto the balls of his feet (knee extension), he will have inefficient technique for two reasons. The <u>first</u> is that he will destabilize his base, like a catapult in quicksand. This will make the lifter slow at the top of the second pull.

The second is that the amount of forward movement in the bar's direction of flight that a conscious knee extension at this point will cause the lifter to enter the receiving phase unbalanced to the front, resulting in rounded torsos at the bottom of this position, very hard recoveries or, simply, the bar dropped to the floor.

Here's how it should look from the floor and right through it.

Sweep the bar from the floor, driving through your heels, the bar moving inwards towards your hips, and as you near full knee extension in the first pull:

1. ALLOW your knees to travel forward. (to me, this feels like the same movement that occurs when someone taps the back of your knees and they pop forward.)
2. At the same time, you should lift your torso upwards, extending your hips slightly. (this is important because it keeps the bar moving upwards as your hips are descending) (YOU CANNOT ALLOW THE BAR TO STALL HERE)
3. With your shoulders still slightly out past the bar and with your balance still through your heels (rear of feet), your hips now lowered and your torso more toward vertical, you have completed the scoop and should immediately initiate the almost vertical, explosive extension of the hips, accelerating the bar from the **Launch Point**

Repeated practice using the correct form in the Rock & Roll drill, which exaggerates this up-down-forward-up movement of your hip and knee joints that occurs during the double-knee bend will help your body and brain understand how it works in an actual lift.

Fine Tuning the Catapult

The double knee bend should start and finish with the lifter still being balanced over the heels or over the rear of the feet, if possible. Some of you may have to go slightly onto the forefoot during this movement because of the length of your legs or flexibility issues. Some Olympic weightlifters go slightly to the front of the foot at this point to brace and then redirect the S pull more severely to the rear but that is more unorthodox and can present knee problems.

As explosive hip extension begins (2nd pull) from the Launch Point, your balance will naturally move towards the balls of your feet to a greater or lesser extent, due to the human form, as you catapult the bar upwards. The amount of shift will differ depending on things such as body type, foot length and flexibility. Knee extension also continues here but is curtailed before the knees approach full extension. You should not consciously push upward through the balls of the feet at this point in the pull. Doing so is simply wrong and wastes both time and energy. It is like a shot putter jumping in the air before he releases the shot. Power is lost.

Here are 3 simple rules here about what shouldn't happen in, or as a result of, the 2nd pull:

1. If you are taller at the top of your 2nd pull than you are standing erect performing your best standing calf raise on the balls of your feet, you are doing the lift <u>WRONG</u>.
2. If the soles of your lifting shoes are facing the back wall, in mid-air, as you move from the 2nd pull to the 3rd, you are doing the lift <u>WRONG</u>.
3. If there is noticeable pressure on the front of your feet before your heels are on the floor when receiving the bar, you're doing the lift <u>WRONG</u>.

Here is one more very important point. If your legs and hips are not sufficiently strengthened, you cannot do the "scoop" well or, maybe, at all. This, will, of course hinder any results of trying to catapult the bar. Glutes, hamstrings, lower back and quadriceps muscles all have to not only be strong but be able to work in a coordinated effort to accomplish this movement correctly and at tremendous speed.

Lifters must morph one last time into a basic machine in order to complete their Olympic weightlifting task. This is what makes doing these lifts absolutely different than any other athletic task and causes lifters to bend the rules of normal athletic movement. <u>They must catch the bar before it falls back toward the earth.</u> And, so: the **Slingshot**.

Finally…the Slingshot
(How the lifter becomes a projectile during the Pull-under)

You must now propel yourself downward to a solid catching position to receive the bar in the 3rd pull. You have to mimic the simple Slingshot, I believe, to solve this problem. Your arms and the trapezius muscles are involved here-some may just use their arms- like the cord of a slingshot, to propel you downward to the catch position. The slowing mass of the ascending bar actually helps you to accelerate yourself downward. The more limited the time you are actually in the air during the transition from the 2nd pull to the end of the pull-under, the more efficient the process. Meaningful change in your position relative to completing the task depends on how much you can stay in contact with the floor during this phase

Two things should be emphasized here. The first, the rise onto the front of your feet is used for driving or shuffling out or to the rear, of your feet during this phase has nothing to do with making the bar go higher. You are past that phase of the lift. This movement of the feet is outward (or backward or forward) and downward and occurs at the start of the pull-under. It is used to get your feet to a wider base, allowing a lower squat, a better receiving position, and to get your heels back down on the platform.

The second thing to keep in mind is that your hips are being propelled downward first, not your shoulders. This may be difficult for the brain to accept at first because generally the head and shoulders lead the way in athletic movements. Again, you must *imagine* that the center of your body is the projectile being launched downward. This will help you land in a squat or split with your torso as erect as it can be and your feet flat on the floor.

Now you merely have to stand up. (Well, it's not that easy but it's easier.)

Standing up

Standing up, or recovering, from a full squat position can be easy or treacherous for a lifter. You must, of course, have strengthened your legs sufficiently to prepare you for this movement but you must also have proper technique. It is very frustrating to shoulder a weight or snatch it overhead only to lose the lift because you couldn't stand up with it.

If you are in a proper, deep squat, you should have your weight balanced over the mid-foot area and your torso should be fairly upright. It will have to be at some angle forward, of course, but it should be no more angled than your front or overhead squat positions.

Just as in any deep squat, the glutes and hamstrings should start the upward motion, followed quickly by the addition of the quadriceps to the effort. You should try to think about raising your torso toward vertical early in the assent. As you rise your hips will come forward easier if you keep thinking about hip extension and/or raising your torso, rather than knee extension. The simple reason for this is that at the bottom of a proper, deep squat, the knee extensors are not in a good position to help you rise. If you concentrate on knee extension here, you will draw yourself forward on your feet and probably tilt your torso forward as well. Neither of these is advantageous to the task of standing up with a weight on your shoulders or above your head.

You will feel the balance move toward the front of your feet about two-thirds through the assent. Try to lift your torso with more effort toward vertical here and get your balance back on the mid-foot as soon as possible. As you reach the straight-legged position, you should, once again, be balanced over your heels. Your torso should be vertical also. This position in the Clean recovery readies you immediately for the Jerk or to do a quick bounce adjustment of your grip on the bar and then Jerk. At the completion of the Snatch, this balance position should keep the bar, your shoulders and your hips in good alignment.

Many, many deep Back Squats, a good number of Font Squats, many repetitions of the Olympic lifts and consistent work with core assistant exercises will ready you to stand with anything you can Clean or Snatch.

Wait a minute. The road-sign up ahead—Gulp!

*****

The Twilight Zone Information Center
(Topics to keep everyone awake, laughing and thinking)

The Olympic-Style Lifts/Triple Extension Myth
(Uh, oh.)

When discussion turns to the relative value of the Olympic-style lifts, there is always a lot of talk about triple extension (in sports, movements that involve the forceful extension of the hip, knee and ankle joints) and how to improve it. In fact, most methods of teaching the Olympic-style lifts in the U.S. emphasize the goal of getting to forceful triple extension at the top of the 2nd pull. In fact, many coaches in the U.S. want lifters to jump into the air with all the force they can muster. That might be useful if the athletes were trying to put the bar on the top shelf in a closet, but in the real world of weightlifting it's the wrong technical advice.

Achieving powerful triple extension allows athletes to perform many important and powerful movements in sports. It is key to performance and the most recognizable by fans, athletes and coaches as a living, moving definition of what power "looks like." Look at a basketball player leaping to dunk the ball. Look at a pro tennis player delivering a hundred mile per hour serve. Look at a linebacker delivering a crushing tackle to a tailback. Explosive triple extension is critical for all of these easily recalled visual moments and more, in sports. And, making the Olympic-style lifts a key part of all athletes strength programs will optimize their ability to perform this critical movement.

However, in the practical sense, Olympic-style lifts, performed correctly, should not employ a true, forceful triple extension movement as is usually defined and is witnessed in most sports. The Olympic-style lifts certainly do involve a great degree of powerful hip extension during the 2nd pull. Arguably, more power is produced in the few tenths of a second during hip extension than in any other movement in sports. Knee extension is very crucial during the first pull is somewhat evident in and the 2nd pull. However, when performing Olympic lifts, aggressive, forceful knee and ankle extension (plantar flexion), should not happen at the finish of the 2nd pull with the intent of delivering upward force to the implement and causing the athlete to continue in the same direction. One or another of these is the goal of triple extension movements in all other sports. In fact, the Olympic-style lifts can be performed perfectly well without any plantar flexion whatever by some athletes. And, that is the final stage of what makes triple extension crucial in most sports and so readily recognizable.

By the strictest of definitions, triple extension does happen when most athletes perform Olympic lifts. But, it happens 1) because the force of the hip extension forces the heels to lift away from the floor, and 2) the lifter has to push from the front of the feet to move them to reach the normally wider and possibly to the rear, catch position. In some cases a good deal of plantar flexion and knee extension is seen because an athlete is purposely jumping backward to catch the bar.

One problem with using a technique that emphasizes aggressive triple extension at the top of the 2nd pull with the intent of making the bar rise is that it makes the transition to and the accomplishment of the pull-under (3rd pull) slower than it should be. And, slow is never good at this stage of the Olympic lifts. Another problem is that emphasizing triple extension in Olympic lifts tends to move the bar forward, away from the lifter in the 2nd pull, making it harder to shoulder (Clean) or put overhead correctly (Snatch).

Some say this is simply a matter of correctly timing the transition from the triple extension to the downward movement, not a major flaw in technique. This is no more true than telling a discus thrower that having no torque between his upper body and his hips is fine as long as his timing is good at the point of delivery. That lack of torque would be a major flaw in discus form and would limit the athlete's potential for his throws, no matter how much he works on timing. Aggressive knee and ankle extension with the intent of delivering upward force to the bar will limit an athlete's potential for lifting greater weight, no matter how much he works on timing.

*****

Gas Station Break

WEIGHTLIFTING COACHES:

Almost all true triple extension movements in sports have to do with the delivery of force by an athlete who is completing a movement, launching himself or throwing an implement he is holding in some direction away from his starting position. An exception is Olympic weightlifting. In Olympic weightlifting, the task presented to the athlete during the pull is to launch an implement, work with it to bring himself back to approximately his starting position and then, catch that same implement, to complete the movement.

Does that difference mean that doing these lifts is not crucial for the proper development of athletes in other sports? O<u>f course not.</u> Performing the Olympic-style lifts correctly is essential to fully developing the maximum power output of the triple extension movement. No other weightlifting movement does nearly as much to teach the athlete about overall, athletic usage of the major posterior chain musculature (glutes, hamstrings, lower back) that is essential for powerful hip extension. Nor does any exercise affect those muscles sufficiently to allow them to create the coordinated high intensity contractions needed in sports.

The quickness with which athletes properly taught the Olympic-style lifts can have complete control these muscles is unmatched in sports. The power output is unmatched. The ability to react under tremendous load is also unmatched. Watch some video sometime of an Olympic weightlifter moving his body from driving a bar upwards to squatting under it to catch it. It is a blur of power and athleticism. All athletes need to do these lifts and need to do them often.

Is the "S" Tilting and Are Lifters Jumping Backward??

Yes and yes. More and more, athletes who perform these Olympic-style lifts are driving the bar deeper into the base of support area. Some of the best Olympic weightlifters are using a jump-back movement to receive the bar. If more advanced pulling technique is being employed, the *S* can certainly be tilted toward the rear.

Both those things can occur, especially jumping back, for the wrong reasons, as well. If, for instance, a novice lifters are fearful of getting under the bar, they might jump back from it at the last moment or the bar might be pulled in such a bad way that it forces them to be thrown backward. And, if lifters completely raise their torsos too early in the second pull, they might tilt the S. But, with more and more use and development of the posterior chain musculature, the tilted *"S"* and the jump-back techniques will be seen more and will produce very good results.

Are Those shoulders Set Behind the Bar?

Again, yes. More lifters are now using another new and unusual technique. The greatest difference can be seen at the Set position. Some lifters have started setting their shoulders behind the bar at the start of the pull, their weight balanced over their heels and actually driving the bar from the floor with their shoulders still behind the bar for several inches off the platform. Not many years ago this would have been considered an unforgivable mistake and any lifter doing it would have coaches descend upon him quickly, invoking the name of this or that famous text or coach that forbids this kind of heresy.

But, as often happens, yesterday's heresy is today's interesting innovation. It seems that along with the advent of much more squatting and much more attention paid to the development of the posterior chain muscles, this technique can be used and is, for some, a more efficient way to move weight when doing these Olympic-style lifts.

*****

An aside: Many years ago a young man named Dick Fosbury, a high jumper, rather than using the universally used technique of straddling the bar with the front of his torso facing it, started to arch over the bar with his back to it. It quickly became known as the "Fosbury Flop" and was considered an anomaly, at best. He won the '68 Olympics. Now, you can hardly find a high jumper that doesn't "flop" and hardly a fan or a young athlete that knows that any other form was ever used. It has simply become standard high jumping technique. By the way, sports science caught up with the reasons for the success of this technique a few years after Fosbury tinkered and invented it. It was nice of them to endorse it.

*****

In this behind the bar Set position technique, hips are set extra low and the lifters actually set themselves over their heels to start driving the bar. A bit of hip extension actually starts the upward drive from the Set position. Shoulders are set behind the bar, although their position relative to the shoulder joint is still forward, down and relaxed. The arm line is actually past vertical and angled towards the back slightly. The bar is placed slightly closer to the athletes, just behind the base of the toes. The lifters still endeavor to achieve a position of having their shoulders vertically over the bar after it has risen a few inches from the floor and only allow his torso to lean forward more as the bar approaches the Launch Point, which would be the orthodox positioning. The movements in the last two parts of the lift are also much the same as other correct techniques. The lifters using this technique will often jump slightly back to catch the bar, which seems proper form for this style.

What I have witnessed is that some lifters tend to sweep the bar inward better using this start position, and the *"S"* is extremely tilted. There is some acceptable jump back to the catch position. It seems to be a very powerful position and the athletes I have using it have adapted to it very easily. Interestingly, it does present a more efficient start of the pendulum movement of the bar inward toward the lifter from the floor, since, in essence, the Set position puts the bar at the far end of the pendulum swing, which causes the bar, once lifted from the floor to swing towards the lifters, making it easier for them to sweep the bar inward.

This may be a technique that can be used by many more weightlifting athletes with success. It may be "the next big thing" and prove to be a natural evolution in the positioning of humans to do Olympic-style lifts. Or, it may be more of an anomaly. At this point, it is worth investigating. My feeling is that it will be a technique that is efficient for athletes with very strong posterior chain musculature with shorter legs and relatively short thighbones. However, I will not be surprised by anything after seeing the early, successful use of this innovation in technique.

What About Pulling and Set Positions for Athletes in Other Sports??
(A summary)

Let's try to agree that the best technique for doing the Olympic-style lifts will be found in the sport of Olympic weightlifting. In a sport in which the object is to lift the greatest weight above the head with or without a stop at the shoulders, it is reasonable to assume that the most knowledge about how to accomplish this in the most efficient manner is known by its participants. The most serious questions about technique and the most creative answers are likely to come from this group as well. That said, here's my take on what has happened over the last forty to fifty years, starting with the Set position. Keep in mind there are other "takes" on this, but this is my book.

Because of the extra strength of the legs and hips in more and more weightlifters and other technical rule changes, the starting position (The Set) began to get lower and lower. The torso angle also started to shift from almost parallel to the floor to an angle much closer to upright. This took the strain of the heavier and heavier weights being lifted off the back at the start of the lift and put more reliance on hip and leg strength, which should be much stronger than back muscles anyway.

At the Set position, balance has remained on the front part of the feet with a shift to the rear as the bar is driven from the floor. I will add here that of late a new Set position has emerged in which the balance is on the heels.
The shoulder placement at the start, once written in stone to be far out in front of the bar is now, for many lifters is directly over the bar. In fact, the only place that it seems that the shoulders still absolutely have to be far out in front of the bar during the entire pull is at the point just before and after the double knee bend is initiated. To confuse matters even more, there are even weightlifters now using a Set position with their shoulders behind the bar and bodyweight balanced over the heels with good results. *(Blasphemers! Heretics!)*

Shoulder placement, in relationship to their natural position on the torso, is now slightly forward and down when performing Olympic lifting. This position also stretches the portion of the trapezius muscle above the shoulders down and slightly forward.

At the top of the second pull there is less and less "air time" by weightlifters. Emphasizing the forceful triple extension movement as a necessary part of properly driving the bar upward has waned. Lifters have competed very well internationally without moving their feet whatsoever. Most really good international weightlifters now triple extend to get to catch positions in the squat, not to drive the bar.

Let's take a quiz.

*****

Pop Quiz

STATEMENT: The shoulders must be out in front of the bar in the Set Position.

FALSE:
Many athletes can lift perfectly well with their shoulders vertically over or even slightly behind the bar at the Set Position!

STATEMENT: The hips have to be higher than the knees at the Set Position.

FALSE:
Many athletes lift perfectly well with their hips either even with or below the knees at the Set Position!

STATEMENT: Arms should be straight and travel by the sides of the knees as the hands grip the bar in the Set position.

TRUE AND FALSE!:
Arms traveling beside the knees is about as close to a comprehensive rule as I can think of but arms, which should be straight for most, can be bent by some in order to "shorten" them, thus getting the bar closer to the hips for the catapulting phase. More elite Olympic weightlifters do this in the Clean. (It is important to note here that this does not mean that the lifter is actively continuing to contract his biceps more during the first pull but, rather, holding a certain angle of elbow bend that will put the bar where he wants it when it reaches his hip region.)

STATEMENT: The bodyweight of the lifter is balanced over the forefeet in the Set Position.

TRUE & FALSE!:
This is a surprise, even to me. The great majority of lifters should start the Set position with their weight balanced over their forefeet. But, lifters who can start with their shoulders slightly behind the bar (and I'm finding more than I thought) also are better served having their bodyweight balanced over the heels in the Set Position!

STATEMENT: The bar should be over the base of the big toe in the Set Position.

TRUE:

This seems to be the most efficient position for most, with very little variation. (I don't have enough data to say that all lifters starting behind the bar have to have the bar closer than that.)

STATEMENT: Your shins have to touch the bar in the Set Position.

FALSE:
They might and they might not. This really depends on how flexible you happen to be at the ankles. If you set the bar correctly over the base of your big toe, you might touch the bar with your shins in the Set Position but if you happen to be rather inflexible, your shins might not touch it but you may still be in a perfectly good Set Position. And, by the way, if your shins are always cut up from doing Olympic lifts, you're doing them wrong.

STATEMENT: The shoulders should be pulled back (scapulae retracted) in the Set Position.

FALSE:
The shoulders are not pulled back in this position. With the elbows pointing towards the ends of the bar, the shoulders should be set slightly forward and pulled downward.

STATEMENT: The head and eyes should be looking up at the ceiling in the Set Position.

FALSE:
The head can be held in line with the torso or raised slightly, facing forward, as can the gaze of the eyes. The important thing is that the head, like that of a sprinter, should be in a relaxed posture in the Set Position. If the head is craned upwards or the eyes are looking at the ceiling, the lifter is likely to drive the bar incorrectly when he starts the lift. Also, if the lifter is looking directly down at the floor, success is not likely.

STATEMENT: The back should be angled and straight in the Set Position.

TRUE:
Whew! The Earth is still round.

STATEMENT: The athletes with the best vertical jumps in all of sports are Olympic Weightlifters.

TRUE.

Time to get back on the road.

CHAPTER VI: Nuts and Bolts

Spotting and Physical Cues

Before starting in with the nuts and bolts lifts, I want to say a bit about Spotting and Physical Cues. The reasons for and the methods used to perform these types of physical contact should be clear before we proceed in this process. Below are the basics. Knowing what coaches are trying to accomplish when they employ physical cues or when they suggest spotters for certain lifts will help you to understand their process and be more confident while you are learning how to properly lift weights.

<u>Physical cues</u> (short taps or touches by the coach) are an essential part of coaching, so we have to have some general rules about it. Additionally, many times spotting is essential, especially in gymnastics and weightlifting, and that is going to bring about close physical contact between you, the coaches and other athletes. Spotting involves assists by coaches and/or other athletes in physically supporting you for safety reasons. Some physical cues are necessary to fix a position quickly-"on the fly."

As a coach and/or an athlete, you must be aware of the possibilities of misinterpretation of any physical contact when physical cues or spotting, and I really suggest to all coaches that tell you what they are doing and ask your permission first, when feasible.

COACHES:

1. Ask the athlete is it is ok for me to touch her/him on the **(area of the body.)**
2. Tell her that you are going to touch her on the _____ and tell her why before you touch them.
3. Explain what position she should be in while using the tactile cue.
4. Try to use the back of your hands whenever possible for the touch.
5. Repeatedly tap a finger along the lower spine to get her to straighten her back.

Only touch her/him in the following areas:

1. Head
2. Shoulders

CHAPTER VI: Nuts and Bolts

3. Lower or upper back
4. Chest (1-2" below the collarbones on sternum only)
5. Knee (front, back, inside and outside)
6. Hips (either hip joint)
7. Elbows
8. Upper hamstring with the back of the hand (most times to indicate hip thrust)
9. Feet

You may have to touch these areas to correct certain positions and it may work better than any words you can say. Athletes should expect it. The knees, for instance, often needed to be pushed apart when athletes are learning to squat to make sure they are in line with the foot angle. Often, with young athletes, the tendency is for the knees to buckle inwards when doing squats. This is very bad for the knees and should be corrected early. You should use the back of your hands when pushing the knees outwards to the correct line.

Coaches, there's not a lot of reason for anyone to touch athletes anywhere else. If you consistently do touch other areas, understand there will likely be some misinterpretation.

Let's also talk about spotting during physical activity. In learning complicated movements, spotting is necessary. It remains necessary, no matter how expert you, as an athlete, become. If it is feasible, you should always welcome it.

Spotting weightlifters during the performance of the Olympic-style lifts can only be done safely when you are lifting very light weight on the bar or using a PVC dowel/training bar for technical training. When substantial weight is on a bar being moved at great speed, many bad things can happen if you lose control. If a spotter is in close proximity to you on the platform, those bad things can happen to him also. As a matter of fact, it may be worse for the spotter than for you.

One of the weightlifting exercises that is often spotted by one or more people is the back squat. Below, I have described ways of doing it safely and some important rules about spotting that and other lifts. These rules apply to the spotters and the athletes who are lifting the bar.

When you are spotting an athlete during weightlifting exercises, there are some standard methods that are used. There can be 3-, 2- and 1-person spots, depending on the exercise and the personnel on hand. You must understand that there are situations in which two or three people do not guarantee a better spot for the athlete than one person would.

There is also a **"Golden Rule"** for athletes being spotted: NEVER TOTALLY RELAX DURING A LIFT, EVEN AFTER THE SPOTTER HAS INITIATED HELP. Spotters are expected to help, not totally support the bar you're lifting. So, unless you have suffered a debilitating injury during the lift, always stay with the bar and partially support it until the bar is racked or stabilized.

Spotting

Before a lift is ever attempted, one thing that can really help everyone involved is for you and the spotters to discuss exactly what is going to be done during the lift. It is vitally important for everyone involved to be aware of what is expected before the lift is ever attempted.

It is also important to make sure the spotters are capable of doing their jobs. It doesn't do anyone any good at all to have a person spotting who is incapable of supporting the amount of weight he will be expected to support.

It is usually better in the case of 2- or 3-man spotting during back squats, that the spotters on the ends of the bar be taller than you (the lifter). This allows them to be in a stronger position, if they have to take the bar and bring it to the rack or hold it momentarily while you escape, if you are injured. It is also easier to keep the bar parallel to the floor if the spotters on the ends of the bar are about the same height.

The Three Person Spot
(Usually for back squat and bench-press and for incline presses.)

In all cases, one man is in the middle and behind the lifter, while the other two are at the ends of the bar. The middle spotter in the <u>press</u> (bench or incline) is responsible for supporting the bar, usually with an alternating grip (one palm facing in and one facing out) just outside or inside the lifter's grip on the bar. The two men at the ends of the bar are expected to support the bar by the ends of the sleeves or, if the bar is loaded to the ends of the sleeves, under the plates. Spotters should use an interlocking grip with their fingers, creating a cradle of sorts for the bar. During presses and squats, spotters should squat downwards as the bar descends, rather than lean over to follow its path. They should ascend from their squat as the bar rises, keeping their hands in a shadowing position near the bar.

The middle spotter in a <u>back squat</u> has the responsibility to shadow the lifter during the squat and, if needed, support and help him stand with the bar. The middle spotter should not grab the bar and take it from the lifter as he ascends. The proper way for the middle spotter to spot is to stand close behind the lifter, shadow his descent and have his arms ready to "hug" the lifter and rise with him/her until they are both standing. This "hug" is to be done with the arms wrapped around the chest of the lifter with the spotter's forearms angled inward and upward, with hands making fists.

Occasionally, the middle spotter will have to take the bar off the lifter. This usually is an acceptable way to spot if the athlete does not rise from the bottom position of the squat and it is relatively easy for the middle spotter to grab the bar while he is only squatting down slightly. Of course, the spotter has to be physically able to hold the weight while the lifter escapes. Use the alternating grip, if you have time.

The Two Person Spot

This type of spot is sometimes used in the Snatch Balance, Overhead Squat, Bench Press and the Back Squat. Sometimes these spotters lower the bar to the shoulders for further repetitions during exercises such as the Behind the Neck Shoulder Press, Push Press or Jerks.

In all cases, the spotters are positioned at the ends of the bar and are expected to support it by grabbing the sleeves or cradling the plates if necessary, as in the three person spot. In the squatting exercises, the spotters shadow the lifter or bar's movement by squatting along with the descent and standing along with the ascent. In the presses, the spotters reach up and support the bar on its descent back to the lifter's shoulders. It is important to have spotters of fairly equal strength and height at both ends of the bar.

Jerk Boxes are preferable to spotters when lifters are performing the Jerk or other overhead work. The bar can be dropped a short distance by the lifter when these high, solid boxes are present. That makes it easier on the lifter's shoulders and keeps others out of avoidable danger.

When spotting these overhead lifts, (especially the Jerk) it is particularly crucial that everyone know his role beforehand. It is doubly important that the spotters can reach the bar when the lifter puts it overhead at full arm's length. That means that the spotters should be taller then the lifter and more than strong enough to deal with the weight being lifted when it is above their heads. Spotters, in this case, must be ready to slow down the descent of the bar considerably to help place it back on the lifter's shoulders, in the case of the Jerk or Drop Snatch, for instance. This has to be done carefully and it is best to have spotters who are familiar with the particular lifter's strengths and weaknesses. The lifter must be aware that he has to help the final process of placing the bar correctly on his shoulders.

The One Person Spot

This type of spotting is done mostly during the presses (both bar and dumbbell) and the Back Squat. The spotter does the job of the middle spotter in the other examples of spotting. It is even more important that this person be strong enough to spot the lifter in the lift being performed.

It is essential that he is able to control the weight of the bar and, perhaps, be able to lift it completely off the lifter by himself, if necessary. If not, one or two people will end up injured.

Some coaches encourage one person spotting of the Olympic-style lifts, such as the Clean & Jerk and the Snatch. This is only fairly safe when the lifter is very young and is lifting light weight. I am not in favor of spotting these lifts past the training dowel (or bar) stage of a lifter's training.

The single spotter should be positioned in the middle position, behind the lifter during squats and above and behind his head during the bench and incline presses. He should shadow the lifter's descent and ascent during the squat and his hands should shadow the bar during the presses. It is essential that he is able to control the weight of the bar and, perhaps, be able to lift it completely off the lifter by himself, if necessary.

When spotting dumbbell lifts, the spotter should offer support at the wrists of the lifter by shadowing the movement of the dumbbells through the press and offering help by gripping the wrists and assisting the lifter in finishing the movement. It is very important that the lifter and the spotter know exactly what each other is expected to do when doing dumbbell lifts.

Pulls (Drives): The Exercise

Pulls (Clean grip/Snatch grip) is the name used by Olympic Weightlifting folks to describe lifts in which the athletes start in the Set position of one of the Olympic-style lifts and drive the bar from the floor (or blocks or a hanging position) to the top of the second pull or just past that to the initial part of the Pull-under. There is no elbow rotation around the bar, racking on the shoulders or movement overhead. Wrist straps are often used when doing these lifts to protect the hands from blisters due to overwork and to allow the athletes to concentrate on the task. Pulls serve several purposes for athletes.

<u>First</u>, since the athletes are not performing the parts of the lifts that are hardest on the joints (the pull-under and catch), pulls can be done in sets of higher repetitions, which allows them to do more repetitions combining strength/power/technique and stamina. They might be the best overall exercise in Olympic-style weightlifting for football linemen. Doing a set of five pulls is like coming out of the starting blocks or 3-point stance five times in a row—with almost no rest. Nothing works on hip-extension strength and stamina like Pulls.

Second, doing drives (pulls) allows the athletes to work with weight that is over 100% of what they might be able to Power Clean or Power Snatch (or Clean or Snatch) and do it for more than one repetition. This allows athletes bodies to adapt and become stronger and more powerful than necessary to perform the Olympic-style lifts and lays the foundation for increasing athletes' maximums at those lifts.

Third, the athletes, at least when they are using percentages of less than 100% 1RM (the maximum an athlete can do for one repetition of one of basic Olympic lifts- Clean, Clean and Jerk, Snatch or Power versions of them), can really practice their form when coming from the Set position and going through the second pull with great speed.

And, fourth, doing heavy pulls from blocks can be used to work the hip extension muscles to their utmost without straining the rest of the body. By this, I mean that occasionally pulls can be done from blocks to work almost exclusively on that musculature for strengthening purposes. Using blocks that are high enough to set the bar at the Launching Point or above gives athletes the opportunity to pull very heavy weight (can be +140%-1RM-Clean or Power Clean) for a short distance. By doing some of these pulls, the hips (glutes) can actually acquire the ability to move these weights at great speed. This is a work level that can't be done if the bar starts out on the floor without major consequences to pulling form and speed. My warning to all, however, is to do this type of work no more than once every three or four weeks.

Athletes involved in heavy contact sports or those that involve moving or throwing implements should absolutely do pulls as they are almost as useful to those athletes as the actual Olympic-style lifts. Most athletes should use percentages between 85-115% of their 1RM in the Power Clean, Power Snatch, Clean or Snatch when doing Pulls.

But, when should athletes do what weights in their pulls, you ask? When the program objective in using the pull is mostly to gain strength, use higher percentages. When the objective is to gain speed or to work on refining technique or to work on stamina, use lower percentages. Speed (power) is the ultimate goal for all athletes in the weight room so don't go bonkers on how much weight can be wrenched from the floor and made to slowly creep up the body. That would be a Deadlift. Relatively good speed with good form is the goal. Work too heavy and it will make athletes slow and blocky. Not many sports call for that.

When athletes are performing pulls from blocks, the higher the blocks, the higher the percentage that can be used to enhance the strength of the athlete. That is to say, if the blocks the bar is set on puts it at close to hip height, the range of percentages (compared to 1RM) that are beneficial to athletic improvement are higher than if the bar was sitting on the floor.

Pulling done with lighter weights from blocks that place the bar at or above the knee and below the Launch Point can also be used as an in-season or peaking movement that can be fast, work on the technique of the double-knee bend and not wear on athletes.

One important role that Pulls fill is that athletes can still do them if they have wrist, elbow or shoulder injuries that prevent them from doing other work in the weight room including Olympic-style lifts themselves. That will allow athletes to keep a good amount of strength and speed until the injuries heal and they can train at full capacity again.

Also, if athletes compete in a sport that puts a great deal of pressure on hands and wrists (golf, tennis, baseball pitching), they can still get the all important work on powerful hip extension by doing more Pulls than actual complete Olympic-style lifts, which can be hard on those joints. That is not to say they should forego doing the complete lifts altogether. But since they are performing an athletic task that overworks an area that is crucial to them being able to compete at all, doing Pulls might more often might serve them best.

Types of Pulls (Drives)
(the Full Pull, the Shrug Pull and the High Pull/Football Pull)

The <u>Full Pull</u> starts from the floor. Athletes can get in the normal Clean or Snatch stance and grip. I have novice weightlifting athletes do these without straps because the weight on the bar is light and I want to get them used to the evil Hook Grip. But, soon after, I have them wear straps during pulls.

This is the pull (drive) that I believe most athletes should do most of the time. It is the most similar to the actual lifts and the rhythm the athlete needs during them. It also teaches athletes, as do the Olympic-style lifts when properly taught, to never consciously slow down after the hip extension during an athletic movement. This is important whether they are reversing after throwing a discus or they are finishing off a tackle or a block or if they are simply going into the catch position for an Olympic-style lift. During the Olympic-style lifts, athletes should always feel that they are moving faster as they go, until the bar is shouldered or put overhead.

During Full Pulls the athletes drive the bar from the floor as they normally would, proceed through the double-knee bend and catapult the bar upwards. Then, seemingly at once, they shrug, flex their elbows upwards and, with knees flexing once more, move their feet from the drive to the catch width, getting the feet (heels or flat feet) back in touch with the platform as quickly as possible. The bar should stay close to the torso during this last part and the lifters should feel they are pulling themselves or their hips downward. Their torsos should be vertical during this downward phase and not lean forward at the top of this (or any) pull.

The bar, still held, should fall to arms length and have athletes support it on the mid-thighs for a moment. They then softly places the bar back on the platform in a manner that closely resembles a reverse line of the leg and torso positions they went through during the pull.

I do not encourage athletes to drop the bar to the floor at the end of each pull, unless the weight is very heavy for them. I do this for three reasons. One is that the putting the bar down using the reverse motion to the floor gives them a good deal of negative strengthening (trust me, that's good). The second is that going over a motion in reverse fashion teaches the athletes about the positions in a slow, deliberate fashion, which reinforces the learning process. And, the third is that if athletes drop every pull, they have to redo their straps, which takes time and allows them too much rest between repetitions. This takes some of the conditioning value away from doing pulls, which is one reason the athletes are doing them in the first place.

Full

CHAPTER VI: Nuts and Bolts   163

Shrug   *High/Football Pull*

The <u>Shrug Pull</u> is exactly like the Full Pull until the very last part. Again, the athletes set up and pull the bar just as they would when performing an Olympic-style lift. At the top of the pull, however, they do not forcibly flex their elbows upwards but rather, emphasizes the shrug only. They also do not move their feet from the starting stance but slightly re-bend the knees as the shrug occurs.

There are four reasons to do this pull. <u>First</u>, it makes the lifter think more about keeping their arms straight and loose during the pull (drive). <u>Second</u>, it allows the athletes to work on the all-important hip extension. <u>Third</u>, it allows athletes to learn how to actively transition to the pull-under with the shrug and to work the traps. <u>Fourth</u>, it is the best pull to use with athletes who habitually bend their arms early. If they are cued to "just use you hips and traps" it becomes easier for them (and coaches) to be aware of the bad habit.

The elbows will, and should be allowed to, bend somewhat after the hip catapults the bar upwards and the athlete starts the shrug. The idea is to not have the lifters actively engage the arms in the pulling or driving phase but just "feel" the shrug start the pull-under phase. This pull (drive) is also great for loading the hips and working on the double-knee bend.

The <u>High Pull</u> (the football pull) starts like the others but is a single, straight-line pull (not an "S" pull) and ends with an aggressive knee-extension position and full, triple extension at the top of the second pull. Some coaches have their athletes add a shrug and what amounts to a quick, upright row at that point. This unique pull is a good movement for the specific purpose of teaching athletes to explode from a flexed body position and keep on driving through extension. Since there is no double-knee bend in sports movements like this, this pull is well suited for this one purpose.

This pull is <u>NOT</u> one I would suggest you do if you wish to enhance your Olympic-style lifting form. It emphasizes three of the major flaws you can have when performing efficient Olympic-style lifts: 1) forceful, upward triple-extension at its completion, 2) use of the arms when not moving downward, and 3) no "S" pull with a double-knee bend. This makes it inefficient for weightlifting athletes and for athletes that throw implements and for athletes that don't often start in a fully flexed position and have to drive out to close to full extension as part of their sport.

But, for football and other sports that have explosive extension power movements followed by the use of a sustained use of arm and shoulder strength and the maintenance of a relatively extended position (tackling, drive blocking), the combination of different types of movements this pull provides is important. However, football players or others using this Pull should not do it exclusively and should be told its special purpose and its difference from proper Olympic weightlifting form.

I would NOT advise doing this pull with overly heavy weights due to the pressure put on the back, shoulders and arms when the athletes try to perform them quickly. Also, if very heavy weights are used, the extension will become too slow. In a driving or a jumping motion in which the only consideration is delivering force in one direction and there no implement involved, quickness at the completion is all-important.

A Bit More about Pulls from Blocks

First, any good training gym should have multiple sets of blocks. There should be a set that is high enough to put a loaded bar at (1) ~mid-shin, (2) ~knee-height, (3) ~low-mid-thigh and (4) Launch Point or above.)

(Sometimes that last one can be your lowest blocks set on your highest.)

There are good reasons to do Pulls from blocks. It gives athletes bodies a rest (doing full movements from the floor is wearing), athletes can work on specifics in the middle of the pull and they can work on speed through the transition from the first to the second pull (drive). And, finally, they can work the hips in a positive, intense way without tearing their backs up.

In, then up, with pulls from blocks or hang

Coaches: Another benefit of doing pulls from the blocks is that it's a good way to see flaws in athletes pulling motion that may be imperceptible when they are lifting from the floor. This happy accident occurs because they don't have that first pull momentum on the bar to help them through the middle of the pull. Believe me, weaknesses will show their ugly faces when they do these pulls or the lifts from the blocks.

The following is a repeat of important information. Read it closely.

Whether athletes do Full or Shrug Pulls from the blocks, teach them to start in the same Set position that they would use from the platform. That means have them use the same relationship between their shoulders and the bar as they would have at the Set position on the floor, when they pull from blocks, unless the bar is at or above the Launch Point. But, have them start from the blocks balanced over their heels. **THIS IS A PURPOSELY FALSE POSITION.**

By that I mean that if the bar had been driven from the floor to the height of the block, they would not be in the alignment they were in at the Set position. However, they should start every pull from the blocks, unless it is at or above the Launch Point, with their knees driving towards the rear, sweeping the bar inward with their lats and driving downwards through their heels, just as they would drive the bar from the floor, so they should be in this relationship.

This is a method reinforcing the idea that when the bar is below the point at which the catapulting phase starts (Launch Point), it should be moving inwards towards the center of the Power Zone and the lifters have to be actively engaged in making it do so. This position and movement emphasis makes athletes work on the sweep and the double-knee bend quickly, without the extra time they have when taking the bar from the floor. And, it reinforces the feeling of proper bar movement before reaching the Launch Point.

Many weightlfiftingcoaches who teach the "S" pull and are obsessive about the "double-knee bend" completely ignore both when having athletes do lifts and pulls from the blocks. Their athletes basically do a straight pull and a jump when lifting from the blocks. Well, that's not right from the floor and it's not right from the blocks.

If the bar is at or above the Launch Point, it will no longer be moving inward toward the lifter and there would be no reason to sweep it closer.

Hip Pulls from blocks are very specialized. Place the bar on blocks at or above the Launch Point and place athletes shoulders out in front of the bar (the bar would no longer be traveling towards the lifter in an actual lift, at this point). Their weight should still be balanced over their heels. These pulls are used mostly by Olympic weightlifters but powerlifters, hammer throwers and football linemen will find them useful as well. They are designed to overload the muscles involved in the explosive hip extension without involving much else. And, in certain sports, those muscles and their supporting muscles need heavy, heavy work that they just can't receive from normal lifting from the floor or even the higher blocks simply because the athletes can't get the kind of weight needed to overwork the hips up that high and hold correct lifting position as well.

Have lifters set themselves as I described above and drive the bar to the hips and (BANG!) thump the heck out of the bar, driving it upwards and slightly outwards and attempting to HYPER-extend the hips slightly while doing so. With weight that might be anywhere from 120-140% of the 1RM clean or power clean, there is not going to be a great deal of a stroke or, seemingly, much speed. And, athletes will find it is difficult, at first, to maintain balance throughout this movement. But, with judicious use of this lift, newfound strength will be developed from the hip-extension movement when normal loads are again being used.

Pulls (Drives) should be done fairly often with varying intensities, generally from ~85-115% of 1RM of a particular olympic-style lift. Repetitions for most will range from singles to sets of six reps, with most sports using the higher range of reps and absolute, single explosion sports using the lower range more often. Pulls from the blocks can be used in season or nearer important competitions. Beginners should do light pulls without straps to practice lifting form without having to attempt the entire lift.

Lifts from the Blocks vs. Lifts from Hang

Many programs for athletes in sports other than Olympic Weightlifting use almost exclusively the hang versions or lifts from the blocks for Olympic-style lifts. Neither is a solid approach. All athletes should do some of their lifting from the floor, as well as blocks and from the hanging position. Sometimes, even within the sport of Olympic Weightlifting, these variations are not used correctly.

Hanging Olympic-style lifts, called Hangs, are done at approximately the same variations in bar-height as the Block versions. The bar is literally hanging in mid-air at the starting position. Rules concerning the relationship between the shoulders and the bar at the start are the same as they are for lifting from the Blocks.

The most often used exception in the starting height position of Hangs is the Low Hang, which is started below the knees. This is also a position that Pulls from the floor may be paused to work on strengthening the pull and for making athletes aware of whether or not they're bending their arms.

If athletes are working on <u>speed and</u> <u>technique</u> and you want to <u>see</u> if a lifter's technique is truly consistent or if you are working on technique, lift from blocks. The blocks offer the lifter's back a rest from the forces that act upon it when starting in a set position at floor level. Starting on blocks forces him to react quickly because the bar simply gets to the Launch Point faster than it does from the floor. If they are using repetitions of the olympic-style lifts to <u>increase strength</u> and <u>stamina</u>, do work from the hanging positions.

Do not expect to be able to work on technical aspects of the lift from the Hang position. These lifts will eventually stress the lower back to some degree, so use them in moderation. By the way, using straps is sometimes acceptable when working higher percentages from the Hang. Light Hangs and varied Block work are good to use for athletes during their "In-Season" workouts.

"THE BIG 3"
(No, the Bench Press isn't here)

(1)The Power Clean & Jerk
(or, Clean & Jerk)

This is the single most important lift any athlete can do for any sport or any reason. Nothing else comes close. The major muscle groups that produce almost all athletic power movements are utilized during this lift. In addition balance and agility are tested to a high degree. Whether you use the high catch (Power) or low catch (Squat) version to get the bar shouldered, and whether you use the Split, Power or Squat version of the overhead Jerk, you will do yourself more good than you can realize by doing this lift during training. It was performed as part of the 10-Step Method earlier, and that was for good reason. It is a basic movement crucial to any athlete's progress. 'Nuff said.

Again, here it is:

1. Take your proper Set position on the bar as described earlier.
2. Use the Clean grip and Hook grip the bar.
3. Drive and sweep the bar toward your Launch Point, pushing upward through the rear of your feet.
4. As you approach the Launch Point, perform a double-knee bend and extend your hips slightly during this movement.
5. Initiate a catapulting movement from the rear of your feet, driving the bar upward.
6. As you reach full, hip extension, move your feet to a slightly wider receiving stance (for most) and quickly get your heels back in contact with the platform, if they have lifted from it.
7. As you initiate the Pull-Under, make a great effort to slow your hip descent by tightening your glutes, while allowing your knees to flex, thereby correctly absorbing the shock of catching the bar.
8. Keep your torso as vertical as possible and rotate your elbows quickly around the bar, catching it in the area behind your front deltoid and over your collarbones.
9. You should be balanced on flat feet and centered on your base of support as you stand up to a straight-legged position.

These days, the accepted definition of the lower boundary of a Power Clean is having the hip joint higher than the knee joint at the lowest part of the catch position.

*****

A Quick Note About the Next Lift

I still encounter this debate about the effect of full depth Back Squats on the hamstrings. Let me settle this, once and for all. Full Back Squats do work the hamstrings as does any movement that involves rising from a seated position. Squats work the hamstrings with heavy load, which is one reason Olympic Weightlifters have huge hamstrings that react fast and don't break. Some people still seem to think that the only job a hamstring muscles have is to flex the knee and can't be worked by rising from squats. They are wrong.

Lombard's Paradox (while not as well known as the time/space continuum) is the explanation for this. The hamstrings act to extend the hips (instead of their usual role as knee flexors) during a standing-up action, along with their usual antagonist, the rectus femoris (usually a knee extensor and a hip flexor). Therefore, they do get worked hard during this exercise, as anyone who had ever done a few sets of heavy, full depth back squats will tell you. If any of you question Olympic Weightlifters about this, don't take offense at the smirk on their faces. They've been listening to this baloney for a long time.

(2) The Full Back Squat

The full back squat is the single most important <u>assistance exercise</u> for weightlifters and most athletes. They are especially important for Olympic Weightlifters, football players, throwers (shot, discus, hammer) and powerlifters. Many more athletes should use this lift at differing levels of intensity and volume during their training year. I don't care if they play football, baseball, golf or bowl; they need to do some of these.

If athletes do not do many squats below parallel, they are simply cheating themselves of strength and power. Further, if they only squat to parallel, they are setting the stage for knee injury (usually ACL). So, do them and do a lot of them. Personally, I would be all for banning the parallel squat from all athletes routines. I think it is that harmful.

Foot stance can vary when doing back squats. Athletes should vary the width of the stance between one that <u>heel width is under the hips</u> and one that <u>heels are slightly narrower than the hips</u>. Each of these will produce slightly different stresses on the muscles involved and better overall leg, hip and back development. I would not recommend going to a wider stance than I just spoke about and I certainly don't recommend a stance in which the feet are very close together. The closer stance is more to mimic the foot position at the Set. In all squatting, I believe that the <u>feet</u> <u>should point slightly outward,</u> and athletes knees <u>must always travel along the line set by the</u> <u>foot angle</u>.

There may be a few times during the year when using the ¼ squat by Olympic weightlifters or throwers (discus, hammer, etc.) is advisable. But their use is only for technical reasons or for a light assistance exercise during the competitive season. Olympic weightlifters might use this squat on occasion as an assistance exercise that can stabilize the Jerk dip.

Young athletes should spend most squat sessions doing back squats and using high repetitions (10-12's). This is to stimulate muscles growth in size, allow for the slow adaptation of tendons and ligaments and to better learn correct technique, which will help avoid injury in the short and long term. In the longer term training schedules for young boys and girls, I see no need to do less than three repetitions in any set of squats. I don't care what a 10 year old can back squat for a single repetition and neither should any coach.

Also, there is not a lot of reason for doing maximum attempts, at any age, in this lift. Two to four tests at a single rep. max. (1RM) per year is more than sufficient. For all sports except powerlifting, the single rep max. in this lift is only valuable as a measuring stick for leg and hip strength. The value of this strength lift for the athlete is gained by doing reps, not singles.

Below parallel, please

Here's how to do it.

Back Squatting Basics

1. Always make sure the squatting platform area is cleared of any plates or other equipment before starting the exercise.
2. A spotter should be available, especially if you are a novice or if you are attempting a maximum lift.
3. Always check to see that the bar is loaded correctly before attempting to take it from the rack.
4. Center yourself on the bar and place your feet beneath the bar.
5. Come up vertically under the bar and place it on the top of your trapezeus muscles at the top of your torso.
6. Your scapulae should be retracted and your hands should be placed fairly close to the shoulders, rather than out near the collars.
7. Take a breath (hold for a second) and remove the bar from the rack in a vertical line.
8. Take two short steps back and straighten your legs.
9. Stand vertical, with feet about hip width and toes pointed slightly to the outside; make sure your weight is balanced over your heels and your tailbone is slightly to the rear of normal.
10. Take a breath* and allow your hips flex and your knees to flex forward starting the descent. (The descent should be relaxed rather than too controlled.) <u>You should allow your straight torso to tilt only as far forward as is necessary.</u>
11. Continue downwards until your hips are below your knees.
12. The descent should be slowed then stopped by tightening the glutes.
13. Start the assent by contracting the glutes further, causing the start of hip extension and then continuing upward by forceful contraction of the quads causing knee extension. <u>The assent should be faster than the descent, if possible.</u>
14. As you rise, the balance on the foot will move into the mid and forefoot.
15. As you rise, you should try to lift your torso towards vertical. This should be done starting early in the assent.
16. Continue the assent until you is standing vertical and your knees are just short of full extension. (You can go to complete extension to rest or reset balance, if needed.) <u>Breathe out during the last half of the assent.</u>

17. Make sure your balance is over the heels, take a breath and start the next repetition.

*Holding your breath when lifting heavy loads, especially when they are on or over the you is something I advise you to do. However, don't hold your breath throughout the exercise. A few seconds will suffice.

While going to the "full squat" depth is really defined here as <u>hips below knees</u>, Olympic weightlifters often go to absolute bottom position when squatting. <u>This position is absolutely fine and will do no damage to the knees.</u> This is simply going to the full range of motion for the lift and anyone can use this without worry, as long as you are technically sound and don't overload when you are learning the exercise. Far more damage and far less benefit will be done to your careers in sports if you are on the higher rather than the lower side of parallel.

The Olympic Back Squat Variation

The Back Squat that some Olympic weightlifters use is perfectly fine for anyone else and is done in almost the same step-by-step way as described above. In overall form, the Olympic variation differs slightly in position and depth. Olympic weightlifters (1) often go to the absolute lowest position achievable while keeping their backs straight. This is to reinforce their ability to get up from low Squat Cleans and because they simply require more complete glute development than any other athletes. (2) Keep torsos slightly tilted forward throughout much of the recovery. That torso position works the back strength a bit more than raising it through the assent would. This also reinforces their backs for the positions of their sport. (3) Feet are usually closer together, rather than at hip width. This mimics the foot position of their starting position, thus getting more work on the legs in exactly the push they will use in their lifts. So, these three variations strengthen these athletes in the low positions reached in the Squat Clean and more closely mimics the positions that the musculature has to be ready for when doing the Pull for the classic Olympic lifts.

There is nothing wrong with athletes from other sports doing back squats in this manner. It could be used as a slight variation from the more often used form, which I first mentioned.

Low Bar Squats
(NOT)

I mention this squat that is performed with the bar down the back somewhat only to say that it is a useless variation to all athletes but powerlifters, who often use the technique in gaining advantage in a competitive squat that will reach just below parallel. No other athletes should use this squat.

(3) Olympic-style Deadlifts
(Clean or Snatch Grip)

<u>Any athlete who needs to produce tremendous force, has to do deadlifts.</u>

The deadlift I suggest is not the classic Deadlift done by powerlifters. The form differs because the purpose is different from that particular deadlift. While the powerlifters Deadlift techniques have evolved for assisting them in lifting the maximum weight from the floor to a straight leg and torso position, Olympic-style deadlifts are used to strengthen athletes through the first pull and into the start of the transition to the second pull in the most demanding of the Olympic-style movements: the Clean. Coincidentally, it also strengthens athletes for driving out of set positions in their sport (football-3 point or 4 point stance) and all work done in any athlete's sport requiring low, flexed body positions (rugby, wrestling, rowing).

Like the classic deadlift, the Olympic-style deadlift will strengthen athletes' backs and legs but it is done in a particular way that more directly relates to other athletic movements. It will lead to continual strengthening of the core of athletes' bodies and to the overall elevation of their strength levels. This lift will, like no other, increase back strength and add to the ease with which knee and hip extension are done in the fast lifts.

In Olympic Weightlifting, it is preferable that athletes be able to <u>deadlift approximately what they back squat for a maximum</u>. For most other sports, the relationship should be much more tied to the needs of back strength vs. torso flexibility requirements.

Athletes should perform the Olympic Deadlift as if they are starting a clean pull from the platform. They should use the same Set positions for both, in regard to foot, hip, and shoulders. They should drive it from the floor using the same first pull technique they would use for the Olympic- style lifts, <u>except for the double-knee bend</u>. That should be excluded because the excessive weight on the bar might put extra pressure on the lifter and because that much resistance could slow an athlete's ability to perform that movement, which has to be super-quick.

And, they should use the hook grip (OUCH)!

Here is the technique:

1. Get to the Set position (normally balance slightly on forefoot) and put your hands in Clean width grip with the hook.
2. Tighten your lower back and abs and take a small breath and start driving the bar from the floor using knee extension, making sure your knees are traveling toward the rear and have athletes imagine that you are pushing your shins down through your heels.
3. You should tighten your lats and sweep the bar inwards toward yourself as well. (2 and 3 together should put the bar on a diagonal drive line coming towards the lifters)
4. Drive the bar from the floor, trying to maintain the angle of the set position to knee height.

CHAPTER VI: Nuts and Bolts 175

> 5. As the bar approaches your hips, your back angle will tilt towards the horizontal. *Keep your back straight.*
> 6. As the bar touches the front of the upper thigh, you should raise your torso to the vertical position, balancing over the heels, and return the bar to the floor, attempting to go through the same torso angles you held at different points on the assent.
> 7. Barely touch the floor and do it again.

Athletes will probably not lift as much weight using the Olympic-style deadlift as they could if they found the best Classic Deadlift form for themselves. However, they will lift more than enough for any sport except powerlifting and it will relate more closely to athletic movements in all other sports, if they do the Olympic-style variation.

The Clean grip variation is the lift that should be used though most of the year for most athletes. I would recommend the Snatch grip variation only for Olympic weightlifters, discus or javelin throwers, wrestlers or MMA competitors.

Do not try for speed off the floor but a controllable, slower to faster rhythm during this exercise. Try to "stay through your heels" throughout the driving (pulling) and descending portions of this drill, only allowing the weight to be over the front of the feet as you arrive at the set position to start over, unless you start on your heels with shoulders behind the bar. Shoulders maintain their relaxed, slightly forward and down position. Your head should be forward and relaxed throughout (angled with torso acceptable).

This exercise should not be done too often. For those in heavy contact sports, throwing or weightlifting sports, once every two weeks is fine. In addition, it should be done mostly during the off-season. In the case of Olympic-style weightlifters or throwers, it should be dropped from the training program several weeks before major competitions and only be a part of the training program for about two-thirds of the year for most.

Repetitions for this lift should be almost exclusively between fives and eights with only a rare visit to the lower repetition range (except for Olympic weightlifters) and even fewer trips to higher repetition sets (except for young novices or the teaching stages of training). Percentage ranges for this exercise vary wildly. Olympic Weightlifters have to use generally from 100-135% of their Clean (1RM). Implement throwers should use substantially less and contact sport athletes need even less a working percentage than that. Athletes that twist and turn their torsos to a great extent and endurance athletes have to limit how much of this lift they do.

Important Assistance Exercises

Front Squats

This is the second most important squatting exercise. It is often thought to be THE squat for Olympic weightlifters, but is overrated as an assistance exercise for those athletes. However, that doesn't mean you should overlook it or underestimate its necessity in your training program. In fact, it may be more important for some athletes than the back squat. It is especially important for sprinting athletes, whether that sprinting is on a track, or a football, rugby, lacrosse or soccer field.

As far as the technique used to descend and ascend, this squat is done in a similar manner to the back squat, which means you should endeavor to descend through the heels and not lean overly forward. You should take the bar from the racks in the manner and direction you do for the back squat as well, except for the placement on the shoulders.

CHAPTER VI: Nuts and Bolts

Place the bar across your collarbones and the shoulders should be drawn forward so that the bulk of your shoulders should be in front of the bar. Your hands should be placed in approximately in the Clean grip, with your elbows pointed forward and up and the bar in the fingertips, if necessary.

Front Squat

The stroke should be from comfortably straight legs, down to below parallel and back to nearly straight position again. At all times, your torso should remain straight but it will tilt slightly forward as you near the bottom position. And, of course, your knees always point in the direction that the feet are pointing, which should be slightly angled outwards. Your feet should be about shoulder width apart.

The Kang Squat

I call this "The Kang Squat" because my friend Shin-ho Kang, former head weightlifting coach of the Korean national and Olympic team, first showed it to me. Maybe it has another name but I never saw it or heard of it before he demonstrated it for me. It is really a combination exercise, using elements of the Good Morning and Back Squat lifts.

1. Take the bar from racks as if readying to do a back squat.
2. Do a **Good Morning**, which is a straight-backed bow with slightly bent knees, to a near parallel to the floor position, keeping your balance over your heels.
3. Sit into a full back squat, staying through your heels.
4. Start upwards by raising your hips first (!) leaving your shoulders in place and return your back to the parallel position attained when you first did the Good Morning.
5. Then, perform a hip extension movement, returning to an upright standing position.

This exercise, which is to be <u>done with light weight by most,</u> really works to strengthen the muscles of the back, hip area and legs in a manner loosely resembling the movements done in a Clean or Snatch pull. The overemphasis on back angle and the posterior chain involvement will work to make the movements of the Olympic-style lifts and other athletic movements much easier. For football players, it works particularly on the ability to come up from a 3-point stance over and over, without incurring fatigue or injury.

The bar weights for this exercise, except for Olympic-style weightlifters, throwers and powerlifters, should not ever be overly heavy. Twenty to fifty percent of the Power Clean 1RM is almost always going to be sufficient. Repetitions are generally going to be between fives and ten repetitions per set. At first, practice this movement with a PVC dowel or light technique bar. It is critical when you are doing this exercise that as you proceed downward into the full squat that you stay over the heels. Going into the forefoot with this type of movement will cause knee problems.

The Romanian Deadlift
(The RDL)

Now, here's a misnamed lift if there ever was one. It is neither a deadlift, nor is it Romanian in origin. Many coaches say it is merely a stiff-legged deadlift variation. All that doesn't really matter anymore because this name, RDL, is what you will see it listed as in many programs written by many strength coaches.

It is performed as a <u>barely bent-kneed</u>, <u>scapulae-retracted</u>, <u>straight-backed bow</u>, with a bar hanging in the <u>clean grip</u> or <u>snatch grip</u> and taken from blocks or power rack pins. Bow over, not allowing your knees to bend further than the first, slight angle at which they were flexed, as the bar descends. Keep your lower back arched, your shoulders back (scapulae retracted) and your balance on your heels.

Keep the bar close to your legs as it descends and continue to bow until (1) you feel a very good stretch in your hamstrings or (2) your back can't remain straight or (3) you can't hold your scapulae in the retracted position any longer. Once you reached any of those limiting factors, return to the standing position. (I have noted that with women, the third factor is often the determining one in limiting the stroke.)

The RDL

This exercise with these body positions and with these limiting factors on range of motion enforced, can be used to work on a variety of muscle weaknesses, imbalances and inflexibilities.

Done in the manner I describe above, I also believe it to be the best exercise in existence for preventing hamstring pulls and lower back injuries. This is one of those exercises that every athlete in every sport should do.

The bar weights for this exercise, except for Olympic-style weightlifters, throwers and powerlifters, should not be overly heavy. Again, 40%-80% of the Power Clean 1RM is almost always going to be sufficient. Repetitions are generally going to be between three and ten per set. If you are an athlete in sports in which a good deal of running is done, you should probably stay below 60% of 1RM of your Power Clean or Clean for this lift and stay above five reps. Olympic Weightlifters, throwing athletes and football linemen can use somewhat higher intensity ranges, but I have not seen great value in going over 100% of 1RM.

If you are an Olympic weightlifter you may want to do a variation of this using the Snatch grip. The percentages for this lift must be taken from the 1RM of the Snatch or Power Snatch. Many athletes (especially women) will have a flexibility level that requires starting the lift while standing on blocks so the plates don't touch the floor before full range of motion is reached.

The Overhead Squat

We did this lift early on in learning the basics leading up to the full Snatch. It is a full squat with the bar held overhead using the Snatch grip. It is taken from the racks or power snatched up to starting position.

Let's get to it.

1. Remove the bar form the racks placing it on the upper back as you would a back squat.
2. Move your grip out to the snatch position.
3. Dip and drive your legs and hips slightly to move the bar to arms-length position overhead.
4. Start the squat descent, staying over your heels.
5. Sit to the bottom position through flat feet and only allow the torso to lean forward slightly.
6. Start the ascent and return to standing position, keeping the bar balanced overhead at arm's-length.
7. At the completion of the set, allow the bar to descend to the back of your shoulders and flex your knees to absorb some of the force of the bar coming into contact with them.
8. Return your hands to a closer grip and return the bar to the racks.

The Overhead Squat

This exercise is one of the best ever invented for all athletes. Athletes that do this exercise work on balance, strength, flexibility and a host of other things that are crucial to all sports. Do not neglect this exercise. Olympic weightlifters and throwers have to do this exercise and football, basketball, volleyball, martial arts, gymnastics and wrestling athletes all should be doing this all through the year. Mid- and long-distance runners should do this as their major squatting exercise.

Again, the weight used by most athletes should be light and the repetitions should be between five and ten repetitions per set. Very light weights should be used when learning this lift (consider PVC dowel or light technique bars) and, except for Olympic weightlifters and throwers, percentages will usually range from 20-70% of 1RM of the Power Clean. Those of you that are Olympic Weightlifters should be able to do at least 110% of your 1RM in the Snatch for a single or a double.

You can return the bar to your shoulders from the above head position by giving the bar a little "hip pump" upwards, while sliding your hands back to a clean grip and returning it to the front of the shoulders and then returning it to the racks. This is fine if you are well versed in lifting but I don't suggest a lot of moving of your hands on the bar while it is overhead for most.
However, if you learn this little adjustment from the start, it will make returning the bar to your torso a lot easier on your shoulders and elbows.

CHAPTER VI: Nuts and Bolts

Push Press

This lift is thought by some to be a close cousin of the Jerk. I don't see it that way but I do see the value of this exercise for strengthening the core, shoulders, legs, arms and improving coordination between the lower and upper extremities.

The basics of the lift are pretty straightforward. You place an Olympic bar in the proper Clean or Power Clean racking position on the shoulders and your elbows are placed in the proper position for driving a bar overhead. Your feet are placed at about shoulder width.

1. Perform a dip and drive movement similar to that of the Jerk but a bit longer
2. Drive the bar towards the correct overhead position
3. Rather than splitting or re-bending at your knees, as you might in a Power Jerk, stiffen your knees, keeping your legs straight and finish the overhead stroke by pushing through an extension of the elbows until your arms are straight.

You may go up on the balls of your feet while driving the bar and replace your heels as your arms straighten but you cannot re-bend the knees. Your feet stay in the starting placement.

This lift can be done from a bar position behind the head, as well. The bar is simply placed on the top of your shoulders behind the head and the same drive and catch rules are followed. I'll add here that this is a good way to work on keeping your torso erect when you're driving a bar overhead whether it is during a Push Press, Jerk or Press. So, in every sport's weightlifting program there should be some "behind the neck" overhead lifting done, whether it's pressing, push pressing or jerking.

Step-Ups

This is another exercise that should be done, to some extent, by every athlete. Since, in every sport, the legs will sometimes have to operate independently form one another, this is an excellent exercise to reinforce that ability and to strengthen knee tendons and ligaments in a movement somewhat mimicking the natural movement of the legs in most sports. If you are a long-distance runner trying to gain some strength in the legs and hip area, you should use this exercise.

Step-Ups are exactly what they sound like. You step up on a box or a bench. The height of the step for most exercises will be in the range of about 90 to 125 degrees, taken at the back of the knee. I don't recommend doing many repetitions with the knee angle of much less than this because they may put the spine in an awkward position, especially if you are using extra resistance, such as a bar or a weight vest.

Whether you are using a bar on your shoulders or merely stepping up with only your own bodyweight as resistance, two rules should be followed: 1) the foot of your lead leg should be put down completely on the box before you step up, and 2) you should keep your torso nearly vertical as you step onto and down from the box.

Alternate the lead leg every few repetitions to keep your lead leg fresh and to keep good rhythm. If, like me, you tend to lose count, do all the repetitions in the set using one lead leg, and then finish by doing all the repetitions with the other.

The lower box or block will usually be used for faster drills during Step-Ups. Using a lower box or block, you will be able to work on speed, agility, balance and rhythm and even endurance. The more your leg is bent, the more the work will be on strengthening the legs. This is one of those exercises that is not meant to be done with a lot of weight. Almost always, bar weights much lighter than bodyweight are used.

Here's how to do it with a bar on the back of your shoulders.

1. Position a bar behind your head on the top of your shoulders.
2. Start by stepping up on a box with either foot, <u>putting the whole foot flat on the box</u>.
3. Keep your torso upright and lift yourself up, using the muscles of the leg on the box, not excessively pushing off the foot on the ground.
4. Descend by stepping down with either leg but be consistent with your method throughout the set..
5. Repeat the motion, competing all the repetitions with both legs taking turns as the lead leg.

Usually the repetitions suggested for this exercise are rather high. A range of five up to fifteen repetitions per set ought to suit every need. Remember, it is very important that you put your whole foot on the box to raise yourself up. I also like athletes to feel they are pushing up through the lead heel, rather than the ball of the foot.

A variation of this exercise in which you do a calf raise with the lead leg and a high knee raise with the trail leg after you get onto the box is acceptable and works, again, on natural leg movement in sports and may help your balance as well.

The Lunge

This is primarily a leg exercise that can be done with a bar or some other resistance, either on the back of the shoulders or overhead. Or, it can be done with dumbbells held with straight arms by the side or a med ball in front of the chest. This exercise also helps core strength and general balance, especially when the overhead variation is used. Warm up well before doing this exercise.

The Lunge is a long step with either leg in which you put the lead foot down flat and descend through the heel, keeping your torso erect, and then through the range of motion of the leading knee and ankle. The foot of your lead leg should always be flat on the ground. Flexibility at the front of the hip of your front leg will also come into play in determining how low you can go in this exercise. The knee of your lead leg often ends up out in front of the foot at the bottom of this descent, which is proper for the Lunge. Make sure you do not put your lead foot right in line with the back foot. The Lunge, like the Jerk, should not look like it's being done on a tightrope.

You then return to a standing position by pushing downward through the heel of that leading leg. Once standing, you do the same movement with the other leg. Keep up this alternating lunging movement throughout the set.

This is an important exercise for all of you and especially those that have to run or split your legs to the front and back during performance of your sport. Holding a bar or dumbbells overhead makes this a more difficult exercise. The emphasis placed on proper positioning of the torso when you are holding something overhead can teach you many lessons that may come into play in the "on the field" performance of your sport.

Walking Lunges with weight (either overhead or on the shoulders) is another variation of this exercise. This is good for all as well, but I think you should be well conditioned before you add resistance to this exercise.

Repetitions for this exercise in its standing variety are usually five to ten per set. Walking lunges may be anywhere from ten to twenty meters or more.

Lunges, without weight, can be used as part of the daily warm-up with your arms out to the sides to balance and then clasped behind your head.

Good Morning

I referred to this exercise earlier in the Kang Squat explanation. It is, on its own, a very good back and hamstring exercise. As I stated, it is essentially a straight-backed bow, with bent knees, to a parallel position and then a return to the standing position.

Let's get to it.

1. Take the bar from the racks as you would a back squat.
2. Set your feet at hip width and put your balance on the heels but keep feet flat.
3. Flex your knees slightly.
4. Start bowing over, keeping your back straight.
5. Your head can stay in line with your torso as you bow.
6. Bow to a parallel position, allowing your knees to flex a bit more as you bow.
7. Return to a standing position and straighten your knees to just a slight bend.

Some coaches teach to keep your knees at that first, slight bend and some coaches say to not bend your knees at all during this exercise. Above is the method I use when having my athletes do it. I prefer to load the back and not overload the hamstrings when doing this exercise. Some disagree. I think either of the bent-knee variations is ok. The method you use will determine where most of the stress will be during the exercise.

The bar weights for this exercise, except for Olympic-style weightlifters, throwers and powerlifters, should not be overly heavy. Again, 30-70% or so of the Power Clean 1RM is almost always going to be sufficient. And repetitions are generally going to be between five and ten repetitions per set.

Bent over Row

This is a good exercise for the back, shoulders and arms. It is usually performed with a standard bar but if you have a special bar that allow gripping with palms facing each other, it is even more like actual sports actions by working with your hands in their normal grabbing and pulling position. In any case, it is a good assistance exercise. I prefer doing this exercise with a grip that is wider than the Clean grip but not as wide as the Snatch grip. Coaches may want to have you do it with the a bit wider than Clean grip to more closely simulate your normal sport arm separation.

Let's get to it.

1. Take the bar from blocks or power rack pins. Stand and grip it with a grip a bit wider than your usual hand placement and place your overall balance over your heels.
2. Do a straight-backed bow with the bar in hand while flexing your knees slightly and until your torso is parallel to the floor. Allow your shoulders to travel forward and the bar to reach arm's length. The bar should be hanging below knee height.
3. Draw the bar up towards your torso and retract your scapulae, touching the bar to the bottom of the sternum.
4. Again, allow the bar to descend to arm's length and let your shoulders reach down towards the floor and repeat the upward pull.

Watch that you don't start extending and flexing the torso for help lifting the bar. Keep your torso parallel to the floor and only involve the back and arm muscles in the exercise. The weights used with this exercise will vary wildly. Some athletes can do a ton in this exercise and some have a great deal of trouble even getting to the starting position (which should tell the coach something). Repetitions should always be between five to ten per set when you do this exercise.

And, for the Muscles in the Mirror

My warning and little joke to all athletes is that you all like to train the muscles you see in the mirror and that paying too much attention to them will at least give you something to look at and admire when other athletes are passing you by or when you're injured yet again. It is important to remember that it is the muscles you can't see in the mirror that determine a great deal of your effectiveness as an athlete and it is the development of those unseen muscles that prevent a good deal of injuries from fatigue and imbalance.

That said, there is work to be done on the shoulder, arm, chest and abdominal muscles and some of it is very important. Here are some of the basic exercises that will help almost all athletes.

Incline Press*

*(All presses that are done on a bench with a bar or dumbbells start and finish with the scapulae retracted. In other words, the back of the shoulders are pressed against the bench at the start of the pressing movement and do not lift away as the movement is finished.)

The Incline Presses are usually done between 30-60 degrees. As the angle of the press goes lower, there is more chest involvement and as they rise, the shoulders are more in use. Your arms (triceps mostly) are worked in all presses. The grip used is usually at least as wide as the Clean grip but some football coaches like to use a closer grip for these presses to simulate arm position used by offensive and defensive linemen. This use of a closer grip is justified for certain sports and also is simply a good variation to use at times. Also, your feet should remain flat and be spread slightly apart in a bracing fashion on the floor when you are sitting on the incline bench and performing these lifts.

Let's get to it.

1. Take the bar from the rack of the incline bench with the help of a spotter.
2. Hold the bar at arm's length directly over your shoulders.
3. Take a breath and lower the bar until it touches your clavicles (elbows should travel in toward the torso slightly as the bar lowers and turn outward again as it rises).
4. Push the bar slightly back of vertical to arm's length so that it is <u>directly over the bridge of your nose</u>.

These angled presses are often done incorrectly. Two of the common mistakes are (1) lowering the bar to a spot too low on your chest and (2) pushing the bar up to a position vertically over the chest. Repetitions should almost always be from five to ten per set for these lifts and all athletes should use Inclines.

WARNING!   WARNING!   WARNING!   WARNING!   WARNING!

Never relax when the bar is still in your hands and expect the spotter to just take it and replace it. That is a recipe for nose reconstruction…or worse. You must always give help to the spotter in assisting you and replacing the bar in the racks.

CHAPTER VI: Nuts and Bolts

Standing Shoulder Press
(front or back)

Still called the Military Press (when in front) by many of us older types, these vertical shoulder presses are a great strengthener for your shoulders and arms and the now seemingly newly discovered "core". It is simply pressing a bar vertically from your shoulders (front or back) to arm's length overhead. Your feet should be positioned at about shoulder width and knees should be just slightly bent throughout this exercise. Flat-footed weight distribution is correct.

In this freestanding press, unlike those that are on a bench, the shoulders rise as the bar reaches arm's length.

Let's get to it.

1. Power Clean or take the bar from a rack and rest it across your clavicles with the bar in your palms and your elbows facing somewhat downwards.
2. Take a breath and press the bar upward and slightly to the rear, ending at arm's length directly over the back half of your head (really, just behind your ears is fine).
3. Lower the bar back to its starting position.
4. Repeat.

Performing these presses from behind the neck will cause the bar to be placed on top of your traps and your elbows to be basically below the bar at the start. An important difference between shoulder involvement in a press that is not done on a bench is that your shoulders DO move in these presses. The shoulders should raise and the scapulae should rotate and retract to create a supportive base. This same movement will occur in the Push Press, the Jerk and the Snatch and overhead assistance work.

Both of these presses are beneficial and should be done be practically all athletes. I can't imagine why you wouldn't have them as part of your training program. Repetitions should, for the most part, be between five to ten per set. Again, the weights used will vary wildly but make sure you do these lifts.

The Bench Press

To most strength and conditioning coaches, this lift's purported importance is the bane of their existence. We all spend an inordinate amount of time talking athletes out of doing this lift and smiling and nodding when an athlete's proud father is touting his son's bench-pressing prowess.

The bench press, while a good exercise to strengthen the chest, shoulder and arm muscles (triceps) is not as important as the other presses and, in fact, because of its overuse by many male athletes and over-hype by many gym rats, it has hindered many American athletes from performing at a higher level in their sport. It is a lift of average importance for most sports except powerlifting, in which it must be emphasized because of its place in powerlifting competitions. It is somewhat more important for shot putters and for football players (linemen especially) than other athletes. But, even most football strength coaches of the top football schools (as you saw in my survey early in this book) consider it far less important than the Olympic-style movements in their programs.

That said, it is still a lift that most of you should do to some extent. Even those of you who might be Olympic weightlifters, who have little use for an oversized chest, should do some of these to help balance your upper front/back torso strength. Repetitions should, for the most part, be between tens an fives, except for powerlifters, and the weight used will vary wildly depending on, among other things, your arm length. Again, the role that these muscles are going to play in a sport is going to have a lot to do with how much you might use this lift.

Remember to keep your shoulders back against the bench throughout this lift. Correct head placement is also important here. If you are lying on the bench and, looking side to side, you are looking directly into the rack supports, you are too far up on the bench. Slide down so that, looking side to side, you see that the supports are above your ears (in the horizontal position, of course). Also, I recommend that you always use a spotter during this lift to hand off and replace the bar to the racks. This allows you to place and keep your shoulders back on the bench and avoids undue strain removing the bar from the racks when you have put yourself in the correct position. Your feet should always be flat on the floor and your hips and shoulders should always remain in contact with the bench. The bar should always be in the palm of your hands and your thumbs should be wrapped around it.

The best grip width for the Bench Press will either be (1) in front of the shoulders or (2) directly above the elbows if the arms are extended directly out from the sides, when lying on the bench. The latter creates a 90-degree angle at the elbow joint when you are reaching up for the bar.
Powerlifters will want to, in many cases, train with a wider grip than this because of the particulars of the sport (1RM goal) but for almost all others, these first two grip widths will be most beneficial.

Let's get to it.

1. Lie correctly on the bench and place your hands on the bar and have your spotter hand it off to you.
2. Take a breath and lower the bar to about the middle of your sternum allowing your elbows to turn in slightly towards your torso as the bar descends.
3. When the bar touches your torso, drive it up and slightly back, turning your elbows back towards the outside, until it is at arm's length .
4. Hold the bar at arms length when completing the set of repetitions and allow your spotter to HELP you replace the bar in the racks.

For the most part, repetitions in this lift should be between five to ten per set. Powerlifters or football players will use sets of lower repetitions more often, and higher numbers than I just suggested may be used occasionally for those preparing for a rep test, such as is used in some football combines.

Dumbbell and Kettlebells

It is imperative that all athletes work with dumbbells.

You should do all pressing movements with dumbbells often and even the Olympic-style lifts can be done with dumbbells occasionally. Those variations actually suit many of you better in the long term. One-handed Power Snatches are a great exercise for working on your power and balance and Power Cleans and Jerks with dumbbells can serve as a lift done to enhance real quickness, when lifting heavier weights from the floor might not be advisable, due to the closeness of competitions. Dumbbell work allows you to work with each hand independently, moving in concert or alternately. This, in turn, will help you become a more balanced athlete, who is more likely to be able to use this strength in more real sport situations.

As we all know, just about every person has a natural tendency towards one side or the other. You are dominant left or right handed (and legged) usually. You are naturally more agile and stronger moving to your favored side. Coaches of almost all sports have a great deal of work to do teaching athletes to be able to react with equal ease in any direction with movement, strength or power (speed) or all three. You should always pay attention to working your "weak" side when running through agility drills. In the weight room, you should pay just as much attention to working with dumbbells, which will help greatly to equalize your strength and agility on the left and right sides.

Kettlebells are similar to dumbbells, as far as the benefits they give athletes. For most of the movements I just spoke about above, I prefer using dumbbells and see no great advantage in using kettlebells for them, although they can all be done with either.

However, the kettlebell is far better for many exercises in which an implement is moved in a swinging or turning motion and passed from hand to hand. It provides a way in which you can work on one side or the other independently and learn how to transfer a load from one side to the other and remain balanced. The kettlebell is perfect for this. Throwing athletes, from hammer to discus to baseball and football will all benefit from work with these implements. And, they are simply put, fun to work with. Using them is almost like playing (and, you sweat like a racehorse) and that makes any exercise more beneficial. So, that makes them of great value to your progress.

Abdominal Work

This is one of the most important areas to work on the human body. If it fails, you will fail. And, you won't even know why. Exercises abound for the "abs" and there are so many products out in the marketplace to help all of you to get that "six pack" that I start twirling around when someone new tells me of the "greatest ab machine ever."

Do Bent-knee sit-ups. Do leg-lifts of one type or another. Do vertical ab thrusts. Do knee-lifts. Do side-lifts. Do the hyper-sit-up that CrossFit endorses (but ease into it). Do some of these exercises every day. And, for crying out loud, don't spend a lot of money on an ab machine. A simple cushion called an Ab-Mat is the best piece of ab equipment I've ever seen and it costs less than thirty bucks.

So, Is That All There Is?

NO! There is a lot more. But, that's for another book by another coach. I have included the exercises I consider absolutely critical to finding POWER and the assistance exercises that must be done. I have given you a Roadmap, of sorts, to guide you through your athletic career and try to discern the valuable from the vapid. And, I hope, along with the technical information, I showed you that you should have some fun along the way.

CHAPTER VI: Nuts and Bolts

Don't get me wrong. I think that you should take competition very seriously. But, if you take every aspect of training very seriously, you will end up hating your sport. And, that is not what it is supposed to be about. Work smart, work hard, compete harder, but along the way, have some fun. That is not a bad way to think about sports.

I hope what I have written here helps you on your **Power Trip.** Good luck and see you somewhere down the road.

*****

And then, there is this. It's important.

Some people get extremely anxious about coaches touching athletes. Consequently, there is always reason these days for coaches to be wary of situations that might be misconstrued by the athlete, a parent or another professional. Early in this book, I covered Spotting and Physical Cueing. I wanted to present it as the healthy, crucial part of sports that it is. In a perfect world a coach cannot worry about the spotting of an athlete being misconstrued. There usually isn't time. Regrettably, there is reason enough these days for parents, athletes and other professionals on staff to be alert for really creepy people, who try to work in any profession or volunteer in any organization, in which adults work with kids. Unfortunately, the sports world is not immune to this plague.

The first and most important thing I say to parents is that they should make sure that all those who work with their kids have had a thorough background check done by a reputable organization.
The second best thing I can tell you is to look for transparency in a program. If the coach wants only private and secretive training sessions with your child, I'd be wary. If adults not related to the children in a program are often hanging around the facility, I'd be wary. If the finances of a program aren't clear, I'd be wary.

A short meeting between the coaches, athletes and parents before starting any program explaining all aspects of it can go a long way toward avoiding problems or misinterpretation in many areas. Parents and athletes should ask for such a meeting at which the rules concerning spotting, private chalk board sessions, rules for road trips, etc. will be defined and that there is something in writing about the behavior expected and background checks run on anyone allowed to work with your child. Don't depend solely on word-of-mouth. Parents should consider it their right and responsibility to have a written and signed document pertaining to coaching behavior, expected athlete behavior and expected parent behavior during all phases of training, as well as on road trips to competitions and at the competitions themselves.

Remember, good programs have background checks done on their personnel and usually have the forms on hand. Coaches should be more than happy to explain why they spot or use physical cues and how they do it. There should be no hesitation in any team coaches talking about who works for them and what the team rules are.

Don't be embarrassed to ask about these things. <u>It's your child</u>.

Glossary

Bands - Elastic straps used to assist in performing pull-ups and other exercises.

Bench Press - Exercise performed lying flat on a bench involving lowering a bar/dumbbells to the chest and pushing it upward to arm's length.

Bent-over Row - Exercise performed in a 90 degree flexed position with only slightly bent legs that involves lifting the bar from a hanging position to the chest and returning it to arm's length.

Blocks - Wooden cubicle structures (usually ~20"Wx20L" and varying heights) used to rest the olympic bars on to perform shortened variations of the Olympic lifts.

Clean - An Olympic-style lift performed with a shoulder width grip and by driving a bar from the floor, catching it across the collarbones in a squatting position and, then, standing with it.

Clean & Jerk - One of the competitive Olympic weightlifting movements performed by Cleaning the bar, standing with it, then using a verticle dip and drive movement to place it overhead.

Cleans from Blocks - the full Clean Olympic movement done from blocks of varying heights.

Cleans from the Hang - The full Clean Olympic movement done from a hanging position along the normal pull line of the Olympic lifts.

Jerk Boxes - Large blocks (20"Wx30"Lx~36"H) used for supporting an Olympic bar to allow an athlete to practice Jerks without having to lift the bar from the floor. Other lifts, such as Overhead Squats, may be done from these blocks.

Knee Wraps - Cloth bandages or foam sleeves used to cover the knees during exercise fir support or warmth.

Plyometrics - Exercises that train the muscles to reach high levels of extensions in short periods of time.

Power - Force x Distance divided by Time: also, in general use, Speed.

Power Clean - An Olympic-style lift performed with a shoulder width grip and by driving a bar from the floor, catching it across the collarbones in a slightly flexed, standing position.

Power Snatch - An Olympic-style lift performed using a widened grip on the bar, driving it from the floor to an overhead, arm's length position and catching it in a slightly flexed, standing position.

Reps - The abbreviation for repetitions; the number of individual movements in a Set.

Sets - Groupings of a variable number of repetitions of any exercise.

Snatch - One of the competitive Olympic weightlifting movements performed with a widened grip and by driving a bar from the floor to an overhead, arm's length position and catching it in a full squat position.

Straps - Cotton or nylon wrist wraps that can be looped around the bar for a better grip.

Training bar - An Olympic type bar that is lightweight and used for warm-up or technical training loads.

References

Baechle, Thomaas R. (1994). *Essentials of Strength Training and Conditioning.*
    Champaign, Il.: Human Kinetics

Bompa, Tudor. (2005). *Periodization Training for Sports*
    Champaign, Il.: Human Kinetics

Boyle, Michael. (2004). *Functional Training for Sports.*
    Champaign, Il.: Human Kinetics

Freeman, William H. (1991). *Peak When It Counts.*
    Mountain View, Ca.: Tafnews Press

Fleck, S.J., Kramer, W.J. (1996). *Periodization Breakthrough*
    Ronkonkoma, N.Y.:Advanced Research Press, Inc.

Garhammer, John. (1993). *A review of Power Output Studies of Olympic and Powerlifting -Methodology, Performance Prediction, and Evaluation Tests.*
    Journal of Strength and Conditioning, 1993,7(2)76-89. National Strength and Conditioning Asso.
    Colorado Springs, Co. Lippincott, Williams and Wilkins

Kreis, E. J. "Doc". (1992). *Speed-Strength Training for Football.*
    Nashville, Te.: Taylor Sports Publishing, Inc.

Lear, John. (1989). *Weight Training and Lifting.*
    London, England.: A&C Black Publishing

Power Trip Performance Training

"We teach your staff. Your staff teaches your athletes."

Our clinics are geared towards the Strength and Conditioning staffs of Professional, University/College, Semi-Pro and High School teams.

- Proper technique for performing the Olympic-style lifts from the floor, the hang and blocks
- Proper form for the major (and some unique) assistance exercises
- Free, one year follow-up by video and e-mail communication

Make an appointment with me and my team down here in Savannah, Ga. for a 3-day clinic, or have us come to your school or team. Either way, your staff will have a better grasp of the Olympic lifts and how to teach them than they do now.

You might think your staff is well versed in using these lifts, but if your athletes don't look like the pictures in this book when they do the lifts, they aren't teaching them correctly. If your athletes are jumping in the air, shrugging through the roof, landing with their feet wider than the platforms they're lifting on, your team isn't getting the true benefit of these great lifts. And, they're going to get hurt.

3-day Clinic Price List*
(up to 8 staff members)

- Professional Team Staff---$8,000
- University/College Staff--$3,500
- Semi-Pro (Open League) Staff------------------------------------$3,000
- High School Staff---$2,500
- CrossFit Staff---$2,000

*These prices do not include housing, meals, travel, etc. for your staff.
Also, if my team travels to your venue, your organization will pay for our travel, housing, meals, etc., which will be included in a contract for our services.

Contact me at: coachmccauley@comcast.net or simply by phone at (912) 484-5842.

Hope to see you and your team.

- *Don McCauley*

CPSIA information can be obtained at www.ICGtesting.com
Printed in the USA
BVOW031437260912

301481BV00003B/5/P

EDITORIAL

Christoph Pöppe
Redakteur bei
Spektrum der Wissenschaft

Es gibt ein Leben nach dem Unendlichen

Die alte Geschichte wird immer wieder gerne erzählt: Achilles läuft zehnmal so schnell wie die Schildkröte, gibt ihr beim Wettrennen großzügig einen Vorsprung – und wird sie nie einholen, sagte der antike Philosoph Zenon von Elea. Denn in dem Augenblick, in dem Achilles den Startpunkt der Schildkröte erreicht, ist diese schon ein Zehntel der Vorsprungsstrecke weitergekrochen, hat er auch diese Strecke zurückgelegt, ist sie schon ein Hundertstel weiter, und so reiht sich Zeitpunkt an Zeitpunkt bis ins Unendliche.

Unsereins sieht Achilles an der Schildkröte vorbeirennen, schaut auf seine Uhr – und stellt fest, dass diese ungerührt weitertickt (siehe S. 32). Nach den zweifellos unendlich vielen Zeitpunkten des Zenon kommen immer noch welche. Der wievielte Zeitpunkt ist eine Sekunde nach der Überholzeit? Unendlich plus eins? Irgendwie schon.

Es bleibt jedem unbenommen, in ehrfürchtiger Anschauung des Unendlichen zu verharren. In diesem Heft wird jedoch eine andere, hemdsärmeligere Haltung eingenommen. Die Mathematiker gehen mit dem Unendlichen um wie mit ihren kleinen x und y. Die Begriffe und ihre Symbole sind gewöhnungsbedürftig; aber man lernt sie zu handhaben, und auf die Dauer werden sie einem vertraut wie Hammer und Nagel – als nützliche Werkzeuge.

Sie wollen das Unendliche am Stück kaufen, nach Gewicht? Kein Problem, sagt die Maßtheorie. Auch unendlich viele Teilintervalle können Sie exakt zugeschnitten mit nach Hause nehmen – solange die Summe der unendlich vielen Intervalllängen endlich bleibt. Wollen Sie die Intervalle mit oder ohne Rand? Der Preis ist der gleiche: Einzelne Punkte kosten nichts (S. 64).

Es ist kein Zufall, dass die Beiträge dieses Hefts sämtlich aus Frankreich kommen; bis auf einen Artikel aus unserer Schwesterzeitschrift »Pour la Science« stammen sie aus der Zeitschrift »Tangente«, die sich vornehmlich an Lehrer und Schüler wendet. Allerdings ziehen es die Autoren von »Tangente« vor, nicht erkannt zu werden (von ihren Schülern, schätze ich) und schreiben daher häufig unter Pseudonym, weswegen wir Ihnen das übliche Autorenkästchen diesmal nicht anbieten können.

Sehen Sie es einfach so: Mathematik ist wie Surfbrettfahren. Nicht jeder kann es; aber dem, der es kann, macht es mächtig Spaß, und selbst das Zuschauen ist faszinierend. Schauen Sie (ab S. 42) zu, wie die Mathematiker Widersprüche des Unendlichen bewältigen (und an manchen scheitern) oder wie Leonhard Euler, der unübertroffene Jongleur des Unendlichen, seine Formeln aus dem Hut zaubert (S. 19).

INHALT: UNENDLICH (PLUS 1)

Das Kontinuum   S. 60

Was ist nach der Unendlichkeit der natürlichen Zahlen das nächstgrößere Unendliche? Kurt Gödel (links) nahm die Antwort auf die Kontinuumshypothese vorweg

Rekursive Verfahren   S. 16

Es genügt, dem Computer zu sagen, wie man eine Karte richtig in einem bereits sortierten Stapel einsteckt. Damit ist das Sortierungsproblem schon in voller Allgemeinheit gelöst – theoretisch wie praktisch

Editorial 3
Impressum 31

Technik des Unendlichen

Erster Vorstoß ins Unendliche: Bijektion   6
Zwei Mengen sind »gleich groß«, wenn man die eine mit der anderen abzählen kann

Induktion: Die Leiter ins Unendliche   10
Mit endlichen Mitteln unendlich viel auf einmal aussagen

Der unendliche Abstieg   15

Rekursive Verfahren: praktizierte Induktion   16
Der Schritt von n nach $n+1$, ausgeführt vom Computer

Leonhard Eulers unendliche Summen   19
Dem Hexenmeister der Analysis über die Schulter geschaut

Die bizarre Welt der links-unendlichen Zahlen   24
Unendlich viele Ziffern vor dem Komma – warum nicht?

Unendlich plus eins   32
Es gibt ein Leben nach dem Ende der natürlichen Zahlen

Paradoxien

Das Paradox von Jules Richard   40
Es ist erstaunlich schwer, eine Zahl mit Worten zu definieren

Der Albtraum des Bibliothekars   43

Muss man das Auswahlaxiom auswählen?   44
Nein. Die Mathematik ist mit dem Auswahlaxiom so widerspruchsfrei wie ohne

Das Paradox der Biografie   46

Sind Sie sicher?   47

Diskret und kontinuierlich

Cantors Diagonale   48
Ein einziges Argument zerstört den Traum von der Einheitlichkeit des Unendlichen – und von der Unbegrenztheit unserer Erkenntnismöglichkeiten

Verschieden und doch gleich   52

Die rationalen Zahlen sind abzählbar   53